# Milton and His England

# Milton
## and His England

By Don M. Wolfe

PRINCETON, *New Jersey*

PRINCETON UNIVERSITY PRESS · 1971

Copyright © 1971, by Princeton University Press

ALL RIGHTS RESERVED

Library of Congress Card: 76-146646

ISBN: 0-691-06200-5

This book has been composed in Linotype Janson

Printed in the United States of America

By The Meriden Gravure Co.

Meriden, Connecticut

*To Mary Stormont Wolfe*

WITH LOVE AND GRATITUDE

FOR A LIFE TRIUMPHANT

# Preface

THE Milton scholar of today is fortunate in his predecessors, particularly in David Masson, James Holly Hanford, and J. Milton French, each of whom brought a unique combination of resources to the unraveling of Milton's biography and a fresh analysis of his art. Of these three Masson was the pioneer, comprehensive in his search and equally at home in history and aesthetics. Gardiner and Firth never cite Masson without respect and assurance. Over twelve decades ago Masson committed the energies of his life to a rounded portrait of Milton and his age. In rereading the volumes, one by one, I find no diminution in Masson's astonishing power to unravel the threads of each writer's background and his significance in Milton's own creative growth, if only a reflection of differences. I have never gone to Masson without a reward of fresh insight and a rounded portrait of a moment, an action, a dilemma, whether one of Milton's own or that of Marvell, Cromwell, Thomas Ellwood, or Sir Henry Vane the Younger.

James Holly Hanford and J. Milton French, choice spirits as well as great scholars, have inspired afresh a whole new generation of Milton searchers. Like other young men of four decades ago, when Hanford was teaching at Western Reserve University, I made a pilgrimage to Cleveland several times a year to sit with him and sense the grace of his spirit and the riches of his learning. His zest for life, his flaming touch of insight, was with him until his last day. For many years I sat with Milton French on the editorial board of the Yale *Milton*, which French had helped to bring to birth. Was there a scholar in America more mellow, more fair-minded, than Milton French? To be with him, as with Hanford, was a joy and a benediction. In writing a book about Milton, one cannot let a word go forth without feeling that Hanford and French are looking over his shoulder, along with less immediate awareness of other watchers, such as Bush, Hughes, Kelley, Parker, Fogle, and Steadman. Nor can one forget the timely help and insight of a great scholar such as Robert Ralston Cawley, to whom I have gone again and again for aid and advice, including invaluable impressions of *Milton and His England*.

It is impossible to trace Milton's life (in terms however brief), without the need to visualize St. Paul's of London and the neighborhood in which Milton lived as a boy. Other London neighborhoods are almost equally important. This is one reason why contemporary engravings, etchings, and portraits in recent years have added a new dimension to biographical search. English libraries and museums are infinitely rich in engravings, and their keepers endowed with patience and resourcefulness of rare depth. To track down a contemporary portrait of Lady Ranelagh, for example, sister of the great Robert Boyle, who Milton said had stood for him "in place of all kith and kin," a long correspondence was necessary (carried on by my invaluable colleague, Dr. Lila Freedman). The search was finally crowned with success, a tribute to the magnanimity of English librarians and their long respect for historical sources, reaching back through the centuries. Unfortunately, as in all such searches, gaps still remain. We have as yet, for example, no contemporary engraving of Ludlow Castle or a verifiable one of St. Paul's School before the Great Fire. But by and large the wealth of contemporary engravings, pictures, and maps has proved far more extensive than we had imagined, in the remarkable collections of the Folger and the Huntington, as well as those of the British Museum and the Ashmolean.

DON M. WOLFE

*Princeton*
*October, 1970*

# Contents

PREFACE
ACKNOWLEDGMENTS

PORTRAITS OF MILTON
1. Milton as a Boy of Ten
2. Milton at Twenty-one
3. The Faithorne Portrait
4. The Princeton Portrait

BOYHOOD YEARS IN LONDON
5. The Bread Street Neighborhood
6. Milton's Father
7. Milton at St. Paul's School
8. Schoolmasters at St. Paul's: The Two Gills
9. Alexander Gill the Younger

MILTON AT CAMBRIDGE
10. First Months at Christ's College
11. The Plan of Christ's College
12. At Christ's: The Circle of Milton's Day
13. Milton in the Public Schools
14. Milton and Diodati: Spring, 1626
15. Milton Defends His Manhood
16. Milton in Love: May, 1628
17. Street Cries of London
18. On the Morning of Christ's Nativity
19. The Plague in Cambridge: 1630
20. The Death of Hobson the Carrier
21. Milton on Shakespeare: 1632

THE YEARS AT HORTON: 1632-1638
22. The *Commonplace Book*
23. *Arcades* at Harefield
24. The Masque of *Comus*: September 29, 1634
25. Death of Milton's Mother
26. The Sad Occasion of "Lycidas"

A CONTINENTAL TOUR: 1638-1639
27. With Grotius in Paris
28. Milton Reaches Florence
29. Friendships in Florence: The Academies
30. What Did Milton See in Florence?
31. Milton Visits Galileo
32. Milton in Rome
33. Milton and Roman Music: Leonora Baroni
34. In Naples: Milton and Manso
35. Milton and Marini
36. Milton and the Phlegraean Fields
37. Milton Retraces His Steps: A Second Visit to Florence

38. To Bologna and Ferrara
39. Milton in Venice
40. Milton's Stay at Geneva: The Return to London
41. Schoolmaster at St. Bride's Churchyard

MILTON AS REVOLUTIONARY: PRELUDE TO CIVIL WAR
42. Milton against the Prelates
43. Milton and John Rous
44. Puritan Leaders Granted Liberty
45. Cromwell's Speech for Lilburne
46. John Lilburne Whipped in Fleet Street
47. Unanimous Proceedings against Laud
48. The Bishops under Fire
49. The Fall of Strafford
50. Strafford on the Scaffold
51. Abortive Arrest of the Five Members
52. The Cross at Cheapside: Target of Fanaticism
53. Flight of the Great Seal
54. A Divided Nation: The Drift Toward War
55. The Opposing Armies: Courage and Fanaticism
56. The Death of Falkland
57. Why Did Milton Not Enlist?
58. Milton's Sudden Marriage
59. Reconciliation with Mary Powell: Later Marriages
60. Milton Among the Heretics
61. Comenius in England
62. Milton on Educational Reform

THE FIRST CIVIL WAR
63. Cromwell at Marston Moor
64. Rising Secular Tones: The *Areopagitica*
65. Execution of Archbishop Laud
66. The Battle of Naseby
67. Sectarians in the New Model
68. The Damnable Tenets of Tradesmen
69. Cromwell Writes to Lenthall
70. The Flight of the King
71. The King's Forts and Cities Surrender
72. *Poems of Mr. John Milton . . . 1645*
73. Joyce's Arrest of the King
74. *An Agreement of the People*
75. Cromwell Suppresses a Mutiny
76. Charles Rejects the Four Bills

THE SECOND CIVIL WAR: MILTON
AND KING CHARLES
77. Royalist Sentiment Still Pervasive
78. A Momentous Prayer Meeting
79. England for the King
80. The Battle of Preston
81. Pride's Purge
82. A Constitutional Revolution
83. The Trial of Charles I
84. Execution of the King
85. Milton Writes *The Tenure*
86. Milton as Latin Secretary
87. Milton's Reply to the Great Salmasius
88. The Battle of Dunbar
89. The Battle of Worcester
90. Milton and *Mercurius Politicus*
91. Milton's Growing Renown
92. Milton in Total Darkness

MILTON UNDER THE PROTECTORATE
93. Dissolution of the Rump
94. Milton's *Second Defence*
95. Milton on the Vaudois Massacres
96. The Death of Cromwell
97. Dilemma of Richard Cromwell
98. Bridget Cromwell

99. For the Good Old Cause: Milton's
Last Stand

MILTON IN THE RESTORATION
100. Milton Wanted by the King
101. Milton Arrested and Jailed
102. How Did Milton Escape?
103. The "Incomparable Lady Ranelagh"
104. Abuse of Commonwealth Heroes
105. Hugh Peters on the Scaffold
106. The Execution of Sir Henry Vane
107. The Plague in London: 1665
108. Milton at Chalfont St. Giles
109. Friends in the Jordan Churchyard
110. Milton Completes *Paradise Lost*
111. Milton and Raphael's *Adam and Eve*
112. Milton and the Tawny Lion
113. The Creation of Eve
114. Adam and Eve Expelled from Paradise
115. The Great Fire of London: 1666
116. The Publication of *Paradise Lost*
117. The Reception of *Paradise Lost*
118. The Publication of *Paradise Regained*
and *Samson*
119. The Last Months of Milton's Life

# Illustrations

1. Janssen portrait of Milton at the age of ten. By permission of the Trustees of the Pierpont Morgan Library. Photograph by Phyllis D. Massar.

2. Portrait of Milton at twenty-one, artist unknown. By permission of National Portrait Gallery.

3. The William Faithorne portrait of Milton at sixty-two. An engraving from Milton's *History of Britain*, 1670. By permission of Princeton University Library, Rare Books and Special Collections.

4. Crayon drawing of Milton, attributed to William Faithorne. By permission of Princeton University Library, Rare Books and Special Collections.

5. Visscher view of London: section showing St. Paul's Church and Church of St. Mary Le Bow, 1616. By permission of British Museum.

6A-B. Music and title page from *Madrigales*, 1601, a collection composed in part by John Milton, Senior. By permission of British Museum.

7. An early engraving of St. Paul's School, not identifiable as having been made before the fire. By permission of British Museum.

8. Title page of *Logonomia Anglica*, 1619, by Alexander Gill. By permission of Henry E. Huntington Library.

9. Contemporary engraving of John Felton, murderer of Buckingham. By permission of Ashmolean Museum, Oxford University.

10A. Entries in the admissions register book at Christ's College. By permission of Christ's College, Cambridge.

10B. Views of Cambridge from east and west. Engraving from Loggan, *Cantabrigia Illustrata*, 1690. By permission of Folger Shakespeare Library.

11. Plan of Christ's College. Engraving from Loggan, *Cantabrigia Illustrata*, 1690. By permission of Folger Shakespeare Library.

12. King's Chapel. Engraving from Loggan, *Cantabrigia Illustrata*, 1690. By permission of Folger Shakespeare Library.

13. The Public Schools. Engraving from Loggan, *Cantabrigia Illustrata*, 1690. By permission of Henry E. Huntington Library.

14. Portrait of a girl, by Sir Peter Lely. British Museum Print Room (*British Drawings*, Plate 214, No. 24). By permission of the Museum.

15. Main gateway at Christ's College. Engraving from Loggan, *Cantabrigia Illustrata*, 1690. By permission of Folger Shakespeare Library.

16. Portrait of a girl, by Sir Peter Lely. British Museum Print Room (*British Drawings*, Plate 217, No. 29). By permission of the Museum.

17. "Mayds in your Smocks . . ." British Museum Print Room. By permission of the Museum.

18. "The Shepheards." Frontispiece of pamphlet, *The Feast of Feasts*, 1644. By permission of Henry E. Huntington Library.

19. Plague scenes from *London's Lamentation*, August, 1641. British Museum, Thomason Collection, E166(10). By permission of the Museum.

20. Hobson the Carrier. Engraving by John Payne. By permission of British Museum.

21. "An Epitaph on . . . W. Shakespeare," from Second Folio. By permission of Princeton University Library, Rare Books and Special Collections.

22. Three entries in Milton's handwriting, from *Commonplace Book*. British Museum, Add. Ms. 36354. By permission of the Museum.

23. The Countess of Derby. Courtesy of the Trustees of the Stoneleigh Settlement, Stoneleigh Abbey, Kenilworth.

24A. Picture of Ludlow Castle, tipped into George Steevens' copy of Milton's *Comus*, 1637. British Museum (C12g34). By permission of the Museum.

24B. Contemporary portrait of Henry Lawes. By permission of Bodleian Library, Oxford.

25. Gravestone of Milton's mother in Horton Church. Photograph by Bill Brandt.

26. Title page of *Obsequies to the memorie of Mr Edward King*, 1638. British Museum, Ashley 1167. By permission of the Museum.

27A. Portrait of Hugo Grotius. Frontispiece to the English translation of his *Of the Law of Warre and Peace*, 1654. British Museum,

Thomason Collection E1445. By permission of the Museum.

27B. "Pont Neuf," engraving by Stephano dela Bella, 1646. By permission of the Metropolitan Museum of Art, Whittlesey Fund, 1967.

28. Panorama of Florence, by Merian, 1638. From Zeiller, *Itinerarium Italiae*, Frankfurt, 1649. By permission of Rare Book Division, New York Public Library, Astor, Lenox and Tilden Foundations.

29A. Portrait of Benedetto Buommatei, by Cosmus Magalli. From *Della Lingua Toscana*, Florence, 1713. Courtesy of Princeton University Library, Rare Books and Special Collections.

29B. Portrait of Carlo Dati. From *Vite de Pittori Antichi*, Milan, 1806. Courtesy of Princeton University Library, Rare Books and Special Collections.

30. "The Temptation of Christ." Detail from Ghiberti's doors of the Baptistery, Florence. Photograph by Alinari.

31A. "Galileo Honors Mathematics, Optics, Astronomy." Frontispiece, by Stephano della Bella, from *Opere di Galileo*, Bologna, 1656. By permission of Princeton University Library, Rare Books and Special Collections.

31B. Portrait of Galileo, by Sustermans. By permission of Uffizi Galleries, Florence.

32A. The Colosseum. Contemporary engraving by Della Bella (De Vesme 826). Photograph by Phyllis D. Massar.

32B. Holograph of Milton's letter to Holstenius, March 29, 1639. Barberini Latino 2181 in Biblioteca Apostolica Vaticana. Reproduced by permission.

33. Leonora Baroni. Engraving of portrait. From A. Ademollo, *La Leonora di Milton*, Milan, 1885. Courtesy of Princeton University Library, Rare Books and Special Collections.

34. Torquato Tasso, by Alessandro Allori. By permission of Uffizi Galleries, Florence.

35. Sculpture of the poet Marini, in Church of San Domenico Maggiore, Naples. Photograph by Alinari.

36. Engraving, from George Sandys, *A Relation of a Iorney*, 1621, p. 208. By permission of Princeton University Library, Rare Books and Special Collections.

37. Engraving, by Della Bella, of main building,

Vallombrosa, 1637 (De Vesme 932). Photograph by Phyllis D. Massar.

38. Panorama of Bologna. Engraving from Zeiller, *Itinerarium Italiae*, 1649. By permission of Rare Book Division, New York Public Library, Astor, Lenox and Tilden Foundations.

39A. Title page and first page of Monteverdi, *Madrigali*, 1638. By permission of Library of Congress.

39B. Panorama of Venice. Engraving from Zeiller, *Itinerarium Italiae*, 1649. By permission of Rare Book Division, New York Public Library, Astor, Lenox and Tilden Foundations.

40A. John Diodati, by Hollar. Frontispiece to *Pious Annotations*, London, 1643. By permission of British Museum.

40B. Milton's signature and verses, June 10, 1639. Courtesy of the Harvard College Library.

41. Area around St. Bride's Churchyard. From Hollar map of London, 1647. By permission of British Museum.

42. Contemporary portrait of Bishop Hall. From *The Shaking of the Olive Tree*. British Museum, Thomason Collection, E185(1). By permission of the Museum.

43A. Title page from *Of Reformation*, from copy presented by Milton to Bodleian Library. Courtesy of the Curators of the Library.

43B. Portrait of John Rous. Courtesy of the Curators of the Bodleian Library.

43C. Interior of Bodleian Library. Engraving from Loggan, *Oxonia Illustrata*, 1675. By permission of Folger Shakespeare Library.

44A-C. Portraits of Bastwick, Burton, and Prynne. British Museum Print Room. By permission of the Museum.

45. John Lilburne's portrait. Frontispiece in *The Christian Mans Triall*, 1641, McAlpin Collection. By permission of the Union Theological Seminary Library.

46. Dutch print showing Lilburne being whipped in Fleet Street. British Museum Print Room. By permission of the Museum.

47. Portrait of Laud, after Van Dyck. By permission of National Portrait Gallery.

48. Title page of pamphlet, *A Decade of Grievances*, September, 1641. British Museum, the Thomason Collection, E172(5). By permission of the Museum.

49A. Portrait of Strafford, after Van Dyck, ca.

1633. By permission of National Portrait Gallery.

49B. "The True Maner of the Sitting of the Lords . . ." British Museum Print Room. By permission of the Museum.

50. "The True Maner of the Execution . . ." British Museum Print Room. By permission of the Museum.

51A. Hollar's portrait of Henrietta Maria, after Van Dyck. British Museum Print Room (*English Portraits*, Vol. V). By permission of the Museum.

51B. "Attempted Arrest of the Five Members," 1642. By permission of Radio Times Picture Library, BBC Publications, London.

52A. Title page of *The Dolefull Lamentation of Cheapside Cross*, January, 1642. From the McAlpin Collection. By permission of the Union Theological Seminary Library.

52B. "Entree Royale de la Mere du Roy," 1638. By permission of London Museum.

53. Third Seal of Charles I, 1640-1646. By permission of Princeton University, Marquand Library of Art.

54. Hollar engraving of the Parliament House and Westminster Abbey. By permission of British Museum.

55A. Engraving by Hulett, *The King's Declaration to His Gentry and Army*, September, 1642 (probably eighteenth century). By permission of the Mansell Collection, London.

55B-C. Title page and first page of *The Souldiers Catechism*, April 8, 1644. British Museum, Thomason Collection, E1186 (1). By permission of the Museum.

56. Portrait of Falkland, by Cornelius Janssen. By permission of the Indianapolis Museum of Art, gift of Booth Tarkington.

57. Drawing from Nathaniell Burtt, *Military Instructions*, June 5, 1644. British Museum, Thomason Collection 669f10 (9). By permission of the Museum.

58A. East-south prospect of Oxford. Engraving from Loggan, *Oxonia Illustrata*, 1675. By permission of Folger Shakespeare Library.

58B. Title page of *Doctrine and Discipline*, 1643 edition. By permission of New York Public Library, Rare Book Division, Astor, Lenox and Tilden Foundations.

59. Facsimile of sonnet, "Methought I saw my late espoused saint," from Trinity manuscript, Cambridge. By permission of the Scolar Press Limited, Menston Ilkley, England.

60. *A Catalogue of the Several Sects and Opinions in England*, January 19, 1647. British Museum, Thomason Collection, 669f10 (111). By permission of the Museum.

61. Contemporary engraving of Comenius from his pamphlet, *Janua Linguarum Reserata*, London, 1650. British Museum, 12935.aaa.24. By permission of the Museum.

62. First page of *Of Education*, 1644. By permission of Rare Book Division, New York Public Library, Astor, Lenox and Tilden Foundations.

63A. Portrait of Oliver Cromwell, by Robert Walker. By permission of National Portrait Gallery.

63B. Portrait of Prince Rupert, attributed to Honthorst. By permission of National Portrait Gallery.

64. Title page of *Areopagitica*. By permission of Princeton University Library, Rare Books and Special Collections.

65. Engraving by Hollar of Laud's trial. British Museum 491.i.4(3). By permission of the Museum.

66A. Panorama of battle positions at Naseby, drawn by Colonel Robert Streater for Joshua Sprigge, *Anglia Rediviva*, 1647. By permission of Henry E. Huntington Library.

66B. Circle of supply wagons at Naseby. Detail from the Streater panorama.

67. Engraving from Daniel Featley, *Dippers Dipt*, 1645. Henry E. Huntington Library, 124816. By permission of the Library.

68. Engraving from the broadside, *A Discovery of the Most Dangerous and Damnable Tenets*, April 26, 1647. British Museum, Thomason Collection 669f11(6). By permission of the Museum.

69. Portrait of Lenthall. By permission of National Portrait Gallery.

70. Portrait of Charles I, after Van Dyck. By permission of National Portrait Gallery.

71. Faithorne portrait of Fairfax. By permission of National Portrait Gallery.

72A-B. Title pages of English and Latin editions of Milton's *Poems*. By permission of Princeton University Library, Rare Books and Special Collections.

73. Portrait of Charles I, by Van Dyck. By permission of the Pitti Palace, Florence.

74. Title page of *An Agreement of the People*, November 3, 1647. British Museum, Thomason Collection E412(21). By permission of the Museum.

75. Portrait of Cromwell, by Lely. By permission of the Pitti Palace, Florence.

76A. Van Dyck portrait of Charles I. By permission of the Lord Chamberlain, St. James's Palace. (Copyright reserved.)

76B. Miniature of Charles I, by John Hoskins. Reproduced by gracious permission of Her Majesty the Queen.

76C. Miniature of Charles I, 1645 [?], by David Des Granges. By permission of National Portrait Gallery.

77. Title page of *Petition of the Lord Mayor and Common Councell*, August 8, 1648. British Museum, Thomason Collection, E457(10). By permission of the Museum.

78A. Walker's portrait of Ireton. Courtesy of Mr. G. M. Dent-Brocklehurst.

78B. Title page of Allen's *A Faithfull Memorial*, April 27, 1659. British Museum, Thomason Collection, E979(3). By permission of the Museum.

79. First page of *The Mad Dog Rebellion*, July 13, 1648. British Museum, Thomason Collection, E452(22). By permission of the Museum.

80. Walker's portrait of Lambert. By permission of National Portrait Gallery.

81. The Rump in the Barrel. From Thomas May, *Arbitrary Government Display'd to the Life*, 1682. British Museum K3551. By permission of the Museum.

82. The Great Seal of England, 1648. By permission of British Museum.

83A. Edward Bower portrait of Charles I at his trial. By permission of National Portrait Galleries of Scotland.

83B. Engraving of John Bradshaw, by Michael Vandergucht. By permission of Henry E. Huntington Library.

83C. A Description of the High Court of Justice, 1648. By permission of Ashmolean Museum, Oxford University.

83D. Trial of Charles, from *England's Royal Pattern*. By permission of Ashmolean Museum, Oxford University.

84A. Hollar portrait of Charles I as printed in a broadside, *The Great Memorial*, May 8, 1660. British Museum, the Thomason Collection, 669f25(9).

84B. Dutch engraving of execution scene, signed I.L. (Jan Luijken, 1649-1712). By permission of Ashmolean Museum, Oxford University.

84C. Dutch print of execution scene. By permission of Ashmolean Museum, Oxford University.

84D. German print of execution scene. By permission of Ashmolean Museum, Oxford University.

85. Title page of *The Tenure of Kings and Magistrates*, 1649. By permission of Rare Book Division, New York Public Library, Astor, Lenox and Tilden Foundations.

86A-B. Frontispiece of *Eikon Basilike*, 1649, and title page of *Eikonoklastes*, 1649. By permission of Princeton University Library, Rare Books and Special Collections.

87. Title page of *Pro Populo Anglicano Defensio*, 1651. By permission of Princeton University Library, Rare Books and Special Collections.

88A-B. The Dunbar medal showing the head of Cromwell, with the battle-cry of the English army at the Battle of Dunbar. The reverse shows the House of Commons in session in St. Stephen's Chapel. Engraving by Thomas Simon. By permission of British Museum.

88C. Engraving by Payne Fisher of the Battle of Dunbar. By permission of the Ashmolean Museum, Oxford University.

89. Portrait of Charles II, from *Boscobel*, 1660. By permission of British Museum.

90A-B. Pages from *Mercurius Politicus*, September 4-11, 1651. By permission of British Museum.

91. Milton's entry in Christopher Arnold's *Album Amicorum*, November 19, 1651. British Museum, Egerton MS 1324 (fol. 85ᵛ). By permission of the Museum.

92. Reproduction of Milton's signature on the Oldenburg Safeguard, February 17, 1652. By permission of Staatsarchiv, Oldenburg.

93A. Portrait of Algernon Sidney, after Van Egmont. By permission of National Portrait Gallery.

93B. Portrait of Bulstrode Whitelocke, artist unknown. By permission of National Portrait Gallery.

93C. Portrait of Cromwell, an unfinished miniature by Samuel Cooper. Courtesy of the Duke of Buccleuch and Kingsberry, K.T., G.C.V.O.

94. Title page of *Second Defence*. By permission of Princeton University Library, Rare Books and Special Collections.

95. Engraving from Samuel Morland, *History of the Evangelical Churches*, 1658. By permission of Henry E. Huntington Library.

96A. Death mask of Cromwell. By permission of Ashmolean Museum, Oxford University.

96B. Picture of plaque on the wall close to the chapel of Sidney Sussex College, Cambridge. Photograph by Edward Leigh. Courtesy of the Master and Fellows of Sidney Sussex College.

97. Hollar portrait of Richard. British Museum Print Room. By permission of the Museum.

98. Bridget Cromwell. Portrait attributed to Sir Peter Lely. Courtesy of B. T. Batsford, Ltd., London.

99. Title page of *Readie & Easie Way*, March 3, 1660. British Museum, Thomason Collection, E1016(11). By permission of the Museum.

100. Broadside calling for Milton's arrest and suppression of two books, August 13, 1660. British Museum, Thomason Collection. 669f25(70). By permission of the Museum.

101. Portrait of Andrew Marvell, artist unknown. By permission of National Portrait Gallery.

102A. Portrait of 1st Earl of Anglesea. By permission of National Portrait Gallery.

102B. Portrait of 1st Earl of Clarendon. By permission of National Portrait Gallery.

102C. Portrait of General George Monk, 1st Duke of Albemarle. By permission of National Portrait Gallery.

103. Painting of Lady Ranelagh and friend. By permission of the Trustees of the Chatsworth Settlement (Devonshire Collection, Bolton Abbey). The lady on the left is thought to be Lady Ranelagh.

104. Portion of broadside, *The Good Old Cause*, July 14, 1660. British Museum Thomason Collection, 669f25(57). By permission of the Museum.

105. Portrait of Hugh Peters, from *A Dying Father's Legacy*, 1660. By permission of Henry E. Huntington Library.

106. Portrait of Sir Henry Vane, attributed to Sir Peter Lely. Courtesy of Museum of Fine Arts, Boston.

107. Plague scene, from a broadside in Pepys Library. Courtesy of The Master and Fellows of Magdalene College, Cambridge. Photograph by Edward Leigh, Cambridge.

108A. Exterior view of the Milton cottage. Photograph by Adam Woolfitt.

108B. Interior view of Milton's cottage at Chalfont St. Giles. Photograph by Adam Woolfitt.

109. The Jordans Churchyard. Photograph by Adam Woolfitt.

110. Reproduction of original Blake painting by permission of British Museum.

111. Raphael's "Adam and Eve," painting in the Stanza Della Segnatura, Vaticano. By permission of Scala Fine Arts Publishers, Inc.

112. From Raphael's painting in Loggie di Raffaello, Vaticano. Photograph by Alinari.

113. Nuvolone's painting from Dulwich College Picture Gallery, Dulwich College, London. By permission of the Governors of the Gallery.

114. "Adam and Eve Expelled from the Garden," by Masaccio, in the Brancacci Chapel, Carmine Church, Florence. Photograph by Alinari.

115. Contemporary view of the Great Fire of London, 1666. By permission of the London Museum.

116. Title page and first page of text from *Paradise Lost*, first edition, 1667. British Museum C.14.a.9. By permission of the Museum.

117A. Engraving by Dolle, 1671. From *Paradise Lost*, 1674. By permission of Princeton University Library, Rare Books and Special Collections.

117B. Title page of the second edition of *Paradise Lost*, 1674. British Museum, 684.d.31. By permission of the Museum.

118A. Rembrandt's painting of Christ. By permission of the Metropolitan Museum of Art. Mr. and Mrs. Isaac D. Fletcher Collection, Bequest of Isaac D. Fletcher, 1917.

118B-C. Title pages of *Paradise Regained* and *Samson Agonistes*. British Museum, Ashley 1184. By permission of the Museum.

119A. Church of St. Giles, Cripplegate. Photograph by Adam Woolfitt.

119B. Milton's burial tablet in floor of the church. Photograph by Fox Photos, Ltd.

# Acknowledgments

SOME five years in the making, this volume could not have gone forward without the aid of dedicated scholars, gifted librarians, and art critics, especially in England, France, and Italy. Often an elusive portrait or contemporary engraving (such as one of Milton's Florentine friend, Carlo Dati) will require exchanges of a dozen letters and then perhaps elude the searcher in the end. No scholar I have known worked more diligently than my friend Vittorio Gabrieli, of the University of Rome, to help bring forth a contemporary portrait of the fabulous Leonora Baroni. Though the search failed, it was not in vain; the resourcefulness of a true friend and scholar was a revelation not to be forgotten in the years to come.

Acknowledgments are of many kinds and degrees. I wish to pay tribute to libraries and scholars who have helped me round out my picture of Milton's intellectual world. I wish also to express my deep thanks to those in charge of granting permissions to use pictures from the many libraries and museums involved.

I owe a special debt of gratitude to the librarians of the British Museum, where I have labored periodically for three decades. Their curiosity and flow of altruism are as fresh and unfailing as the return of spring to the Devonshire meadows or the banks of reedy Cam. I am indebted for many years of timely help from such scholars and friends there as Dr. Cyril Wright, Mr. Richard Bancroft, Mr. Peter Meade, Mr. Albert White, Mrs. Margaret Smith, Mr. Arthur Commins. These workers carry on a great tradition of service to the scholarly world and a profound respect for the vast and varied resources with which they deal. Over one-third of the pictures of this book were gathered from the British Museum. Where else would one find such unparalleled riches as those of the Thomason Collection, brought together over thirty-five decades ago by one man's foresight and respect for historical sources; a man who sent out his servants each day for years to gather up the newest pamphlets from the stalls in St. Paul's Churchyard? George Thomason (a friend of Milton) was a friend to scholars of centuries to come; his example is not lost upon the men who now minister each season to searching minds from many countries.

On the American side I have had the good fortune to spend several stays at the Huntington Library at San Marino, a haven of many riches, including a wide range of seventeenth-century holdings in both pictures and pamphlets. The hospitality there of such friends and resourceful consultants as Mary Isabel Fry, John Steadman, Mrs. Margaret Davies, and Dr. and Mrs. French Fogle, lends a beneficent glow to scholarly quest and the clash of fine minds. The resources of the Huntington are a revelation of choice selections of masterpieces in literature, art, and social ideas, in a setting uniquely beautiful and serene.

I am especially indebted to my gifted colleague, Dr. Lila Freedman, who has tracked down many of the most timely and valuable pictures in this volume, searching in many libraries and writing hundreds of letters over the past three and a half years. She possesses an uncanny sense of contemporary sources and artists that ought to exist in the seventeenth century, given the historical happenings and personalities that the intellectual world created or took note of. But she has given invaluable aid also in historical and biographical situations in which the scholar is wise to speak cautiously in the face of ambivalent or qualifying evidence. Moreover, Dr. Freedman possesses a remarkable scholarly patience, gentleness, and fortitude that inspire her colleagues wherever she teaches or searches. Time after time I have sought her discerning judgment, and never in vain.

In my associations with Princeton University Press, I am especially indebted to Mrs. James Holly Hanford, who first proposed this volume; to Herbert S. Bailey, Jr., Director, and Miss R. Miriam Brokaw, Associate Director, for their consistent and imaginative help; and to P. J. Conkwright for his design of the book and his arrangement of the pictures.

Don M. Wolfe

Princeton, N.J.
June, 1971

# Portraits of Milton

## 1. Milton as a Boy of Ten

WHEN Milton was only ten, his portrait was painted by Cornelius Janssen. The boy Milton looks out at us, sober and confident, with short blond hair and wide-spaced gray eyes. At that time, writes John Aubrey, Milton's private schoolmaster was "a Puritan, in Essex, who cutt his [Milton's] haire short." This master was Thomas Young, to whom Milton was singularly devoted; later he wrote to Young: "I call God to witness how much in the light of a Father I regard you." At age ten Milton was already a student at St. Paul's, having entered probably in 1615. At age ten, writes Aubrey, he was even "then a poet." Praised by friends and teachers, Milton from youth onward was his own best critic. His earliest verses were more derivative than original. Unlike the incandescent mind of Shakespeare, Milton's genius unfolded slowly, contented at first with small gains of unique imagery and rhythms.

## 2. Milton at Twenty-One

On Milton's twenty-first birthday, December 9, 1629, he was still a student at Christ's College. His poetic talents had flowered year by year; slowly but surely his confidence in his powers had unfolded. In this particular December he had written "On the Morning of Christ's Nativity," a poem he was to place first in his *Poems* of 1645. Milton's countenance in this portrait reflects an idealism he believed inseparable from lofty achievement. "He who would not be frustrate in his hope to write hereafter in laudable things," he was to write in *An Apology against a Pamphlet*, "ought him selfe to bee a true Poem, that is, a composition, and patterne of the best and honourablest things." Milton was now a little under middle height, his body beautifully proportioned, his complexion fair, his eyes a dark gray. As the portrait shows, he wore his hair shoulder length, a significant deviation from both the aristocratic and the Puritan extremes.

## 3. The Faithorne Portrait

WHEN Milton was sixty-two, William Faithorne engraved Milton's portrait for the frontispiece of *History of Britain* (1670). The sightless eyes of the poet look out at us from an oval frame, his face turned slightly to the right. He is wearing a black cape over his waistcoat, which is adorned by a white collar. His curled hair falls lightly over his shoulders. The expression in the lined face is a mingling of sadness and composure, accentuated, as Masson writes, by "the great rings of eye-socket." All accounts agree that Faithorne was able to concentrate in this portrait the essence of Milton's appearance and expression, three years after the publication of *Paradise Lost*.

4

## 4. The Princeton Portrait

THE first mention of the crayon portrait of Milton, now known as the Princeton Portrait, is found in George Vertue's notebook in his entry of August 10, 1721: "I saw Mrs. Clarke [Deborah]. the only surviving daughter of Milton the Poet. she now is 70 years. Old. I carry'd with me several portraits of his picture." By 1734 the pastel drawing was in the hands of Jonathan Richardson, who tells a somewhat more elaborate story of what was evidently Vertue's meeting with Deborah, thirteen years before. At the moment described, Deborah was shown several likenesses of her father, but she gave no hint of recognition. When the crayon portrait was shown her, however, she was ecstatic: " 'Tis My Father! . . . I see him! 'tis Him! and then She put her Hands to several Parts of Her Face, 'tis the very Man! Here, Here-" Gradually the crayon portrait surpassed in appeal the Faithorne engraving of 1670, perhaps because the colors of Milton's face, hair, and eyes are so remarkably expressive. The definitive study by John Rupert Martin, *The Portrait of John Milton at Princeton* (1961), makes it all but certain that Faithorne created the pastel drawing, whether before or after his execution of the engraved portrait for the *History of Britain*.

# Boyhood Years in London

## 5. The Bread Street Neighborhood

MILTON was born in his father's home in Bread Street, London, December 9, 1608. Both the church of St. Mary Le Bow, where he was baptized, and St. Giles Cripplegate, where he was buried, were only a few minutes' walk away. The spire of St. Paul's towered over the neighborhood, St. Paul's School in its shadow. Only a few blocks away from Milton's home, Shakespeare, now forty-four, had acted in his own plays at the second Blackfriars Theatre. In 1608 Bacon was forty-seven, Ben Jonson thirty-five, John Donne thirty-six, William Harvey thirty, Henry Lawes a boy of twelve, Oliver Cromwell a boy of nine. Unlike Shakespeare, Milton left rich and illuminating impressions of his early life. "I was born at London," he wrote in *Second Defence*, "of an honest family; my father was distinguished by the undeviating integrity of his life; my mother, by the esteem in which she was held, and the alms which she bestowed. My father destined me from a child to the pursuits of literature; and my appetite for knowledge was so voracious, that, from twelve years of age, I hardly ever left my studies, or went to bed before midnight. This primarily led to my loss of sight." How much Milton loved Shakespeare even as a youth is revealed in his poem "On Shakespear. 1630," which appeared in the second folio of 1632. The tone of the poem suggests a long familiarity with Shakespeare even at the age of twenty-two. It is hard to imagine that Milton and his father never attended a Shakespearian play so near at hand as the Blackfriars. Yet no record has come down of Milton's attendance at any of the great tragedies acted out within a short walk from his house on Bread Street.

## 6. Milton's Father

MILTON's father, son of a yeoman farmer named Richard Milton, was born in the parish of Stanton St. John, five miles from Oxford, in 1563. Richard Milton (born and reared an Anglican but converted to Catholicism about 1582) had inherited a small property in 1561. Unlike a gentleman landowner, a yeoman farmer was not above working his land with his own hands; Richard Milton, the poet's grandfather, was such a man. He was economically independent and, unlike a tenant farmer, was expected to vote on election day. It was easy for such a man to rise

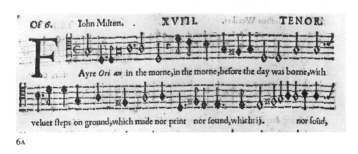

6A

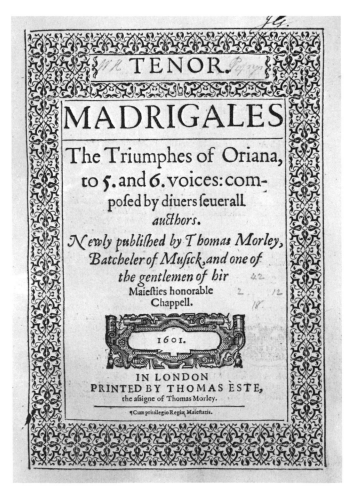

6B

in the social scale and from time to time become acquainted with learned people from the various Oxford colleges nearby. In any event, Richard Milton's son John, father of the poet, was admitted to Christ Church choir when he was about ten years old. A place in the choir assured John Milton the elder of a number of years of general education (in addition to this musical education) at the expense of Christ Church. It was then a natural step for a bright youngster to be admitted to the College. It is true that no record exists at Christ Church of John Milton's matriculation, but as Brennecke points out, records of that day were badly kept, and Aubrey's flat statement, "He [the elder Milton] was brought-up at the University of Oxon, at Christ Church," is the best evidence available. Certainly the elder Milton spent a number of impressionable years in Oxford from age ten to about age twenty; he could not have escaped many influences that helped shape his aspirations for his own creative efforts and those of his son. In his last year at Oxford the poet's father composed an *In Nomine* of forty parts for the occasion of the visit to Oxford of Prince Albertus Alasco of Poland. This composition, in which each of forty voices or instruments had a simultaneous independent part, was, as Brennecke points out, "an almost incredible feat for an amateur composer." Upon his withdrawal from Oxford after a quarrel with his father, the poet's father removed to London, where he met many amateur composers like himself and continued to compose music for many years, contributing to several distinguished collections of music, among them Thomas Morley's *The Triumphs of Oriana* (1601); the unpublished *Tristitiae Remedium* (1616), edited by Thomas Myriell; another, Thomas Ravenscroft's *Whole Book of Psalms* (1621). Meanwhile John Milton had grown into a father of such remarkable gentleness and insight as to earn his son's lifelong gratitude.

"My father," wrote Milton, "destined me from a child to the pursuits of literature." His father's imaginative guidance had helped to unfold a great talent: "After I had from my first yeeres by the ceaselesse diligence and care of my father, whom God recompence, bin exercis'd to the tongues, and some sciences, as my age would suffer, by sundry masters both . . . at home and at the schools, it was found that whether ought was impos'd me by them that had the overlooking, or betak'n to of mine own choise in English, or other tongue, prosing or versing, but chiefly this latter, the stile by certain vital signes it had, was likely to live." In *Ad Patrem* Milton addresses his father as a fellow votary of the muses who has guided his son at every step toward enrichment of his talents and aspirations: sending him into the countryside, away from the din of the city and the pursuit of wealth, making it possible for him to drink in nature's beauties and learn new languages; instilling in him ideals and spiritual strength that made him oblivious to meanness and calumny.

## 7. Milton at St. Paul's School

FROM his earliest years Milton was familiar with the sight of St. Paul's School, which stood in the northeast corner of St. Paul's Churchyard, facing the street called Olde Change. Built of stone, the school consisted of three parts, a central building of one story (which housed one large classroom), and an attached building of several stories on each side of the central edifice. The whole structure was 122 feet long. St. Paul's was a day school designed for 153 pupils; tuition was free. Established by John Colet in 1514, the school and many of its graduates were already renowned; its headmasters on the whole had been men of remarkable ability. The core academic requirement was eight years of Latin and four years of Greek. As it was to do in later eras, St. Paul's from the beginning prepared its boys for Cambridge and Oxford. School began at seven each morning with a chapter from the Bible and set prayers in Latin. Greek and Latin grammar were studied in the morning, Greek and Latin authors in the afternoon: Greek emphasized in later years, Latin in the earlier ones. On four days each week a written exercise based on the readings was required, such as "a Psalm to turn into Latin Verse," "a story in Heathen Gods to be turned into Latin," "a Divine Theme," "a Morall Theme." According to tradition, when Alexander Gill, senior, who was headmaster from 1608 to 1635, assigned a verse theme to write on the miracle at Cana, Milton wrote, "The conscious water saw its God and blushed." The assignment itself shows that originality of poetic expression was cherished in the school; every boy was expected to write verse while analyzing the great Biblical passages and the great minds of Greece and Rome. The mingling of Greek and Hebraic in Milton's background, which was to find pervasive expression on almost every page of *Paradise Lost*, was intensified day by day in St. Paul's school. The fables of Greece and Rome and the classics of Euripides, Pindar, Homer, Virgil, Plutarch, stamped themselves irretrievably on his eager mind. As he later wrote to Philaras, "I have been from boyhood an especial worshipper of all bearing the Greek name, and of your Athens in chief." By the last year of St. Paul's could Milton have addressed an Athenian audience as easily as St. Paul spoke to the Greeks of Corinth? This is doubtful, but all authorities agree on Milton's astonishing facility in the speaking of languages other than English. Milton wrote in *Ad Patrem* that he had "gained command of . . . the lofty language of the eloquent Greeks."

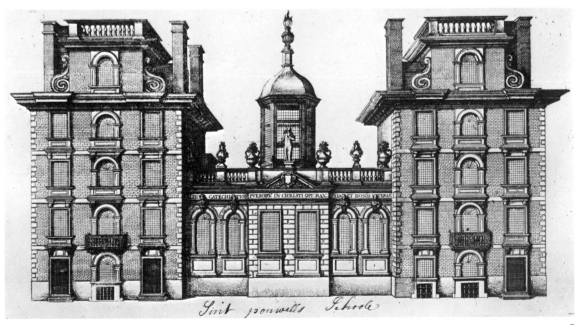

*Sint gronuells Schoole*

## 8. Schoolmasters at St. Paul's:
## The Two Gills

OF THE four teachers at St. Paul's, two had an important influence on Milton's life, the two Alexander Gills, father and son. Milton does not mention William Sound and Oliver Smythe, who taught him in the lower forms as Surmaster and Under Usher. As High Master of St. Paul's, Alexander Gill was a quiet, patient man (though given to fits of flogging) of distinguished scholarly attainments in the fields of logic, grammar, prosody, and phonetics, as shown in *Logonomia Anglica*, published in Latin in 1619. In 1635 appeared in English his *Sacred Philosophy of the Holy Scripture*, a strongly rational defense of Anglican orthodoxy, on which he had been working many years. Though Milton was to reject many elements of this orthodoxy, his affirmation of free will was a link with both Anglicanism and Catholicism, a central theological position that no staunch Calvinist could accept. A strong philosophy of rationalism pervaded the elder Gill's classroom. His teaching of aesthetic principles was also rationalistic, allowing but few impressionistic analyses, even in creative writing. Spenser was his favorite poet, to him the English Homer. The progression taught in his classes was always from the classical model to the imitation, imitation of form such as simile for simile, meter for meter, personification for personification, elegy for elegy, oration for oration, with originality of expression encouraged within the framework of the model. Imitating "the smooth Elegiack Poets" Milton found "agreeable to natures part" of himself. Under the elder Gill's guidance Milton learned that such imitation of poetic expression, as the years advanced, yielded to originality of diction and rhythm, the golden end of poetic strivings.

# LOGONOMIA
## ANGLICA.
### QVA GENTIS SERMO FACI-
### LIVS ADDISCITVR.

Conſcripta ab ALEXANDRO GIL
Paulinæ Scholæ Magiſtro
Primario.

LONDINI
Excudit *Iohannes Beale.*
1619.

## 9. Alexander Gill the Younger

THE younger Gill, who became a teacher at St. Paul's in 1619, when he was twenty-two, a graduate of Trinity College, Oxford, was a seminal force in Milton's development, as his later letters to Gill were to reveal. Unlike his scholarly father, young Alexander already possessed a reputation for poetic talent, beginning in 1612 with a Latin threnody published on the occasion of Prince Henry's death. This confident (even boastful) young teacher possessed those poetic powers that Milton already hoped to make his own. As Anthony à Wood writes, young Gill was "of an unsettled and inconstant temper," but Milton remained his loyal admirer over the years. Gill was somewhat of a political rebel. When the Duke of Buckingham was assassinated by John Felton on August 23, 1628, a wave of enthusiasm from "bishop to beggar" passed over England; the Duke was hated for his failures in war and his persuasion with both James and young

Charles I. Soon after the assassination, when young Gill was drinking Felton's health in a tavern near Trinity College, he made treasonable remarks, such as "he had oftentimes had a mind to do the same thing upon the Duke, but for fear of hanging." Informed upon and arrested in his schoolroom at St. Paul's on September 4, young Gill was thrust into prison. As a punishment he might have lost his ears (one at Oxford and one at London) had it not been for the intercession of the elder Gill, who pleaded upon his knees with Archbishop Laud for leniency toward his son. The young man finally signed a penitent confession of his wrongdoing, was released from prison, and received a pardon November 30, 1630. During the time of his arrest and imprisonment, there was no recorded letter of sympathy from John Milton, but the two men remained friends. Milton next wrote to young Gill December 4, 1634, warmly praising verses Gill had sent to him.

*The liuely Portraiture of Iohn Felton who most Miserably Kild The right Honoᵇˡᵉ GEORGE VILLEIRS Duke of Buckingham, August y̆ 23 1628.*

# Milton at Cambridge

## 10. First Months at Christ's College

MILTON was admitted to Christ's College on February 12, 1625, two months after his seventeenth birthday. After enrolling his name in the college books, choosing his rooms (with perhaps the concurrence of a roommate), and staying on a week or two, he apparently returned home for a holiday, as was the custom. He was a free man now, at least free in the afternoons from academic requirements, though never free from his stern creative conscience; free to meet and talk with brilliant contemporaries, not only at his own college but at fifteen other colleges as well, graced with beautiful libraries, chapels, and grassy courts, many of them overlooking the slow-moving waters of "reedy Cam." Of the sixteen colleges Peterhouse was the oldest (founded

1257), Christ's one of the youngest (1505). In a town of ten thousand citizens, the colleges housed about three thousand fellows and students. Why the elder Milton and his son chose Christ's (or Cambridge instead of Oxford) is unknown. It was not strongly Puritan, like Emmanuel, or so rich in beautiful buildings or renowned fellows as Trinity or King's. Milton returned to Christ's College from his holiday in London in time for university matriculation on April 9, 1625. On that day Milton must have appeared in person before the registrar, Mr. Tabor, who enrolled his name as lesser pensioner in the university books, along with the names of two men Milton already knew, Robert Port and Robert Bell. Of the forty-three men admitted to Christ's College that spring, we have no record that Milton became an intimate with any one as he had already done with the younger Gill and Charles Diodati. He was reserved, full of dreams, a lover of chastity, imbued with a profound self-reverence. Meanwhile, on March 27, 1625, occurred an event full of portent for Milton and all the patriotic young men of his generation, whether Puritan or absolutist in outlook: upon the death of James I, his son Charles I, twenty-four years old, ascended the throne of England.

10A

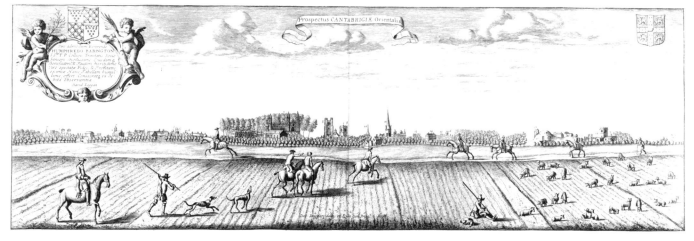

10B

## 11. The Plan of Christ's College

As SHOWN in the Loggan engraving reproduced here, the main buildings of Christ's College in Milton's day (as in ours) rose on four sides of the grassy court, above which loomed a tower with four turrets, originally designed for defense against attackers. Once inside the gate, Milton would have turned left to reach his rooms, which were on the second floor of the dormitory wing to the left. Beyond the dormitory stood the chapel, at the corner of the court to the far left. To the right of the chapel stood the dining hall, graced by a long oriel window. The right-hand wing of the college buildings was taken up with students' and tutors' rooms. If one were standing just inside the porter's gate, facing the court, he would turn sharp right to reach the library and the offices of the librarians.

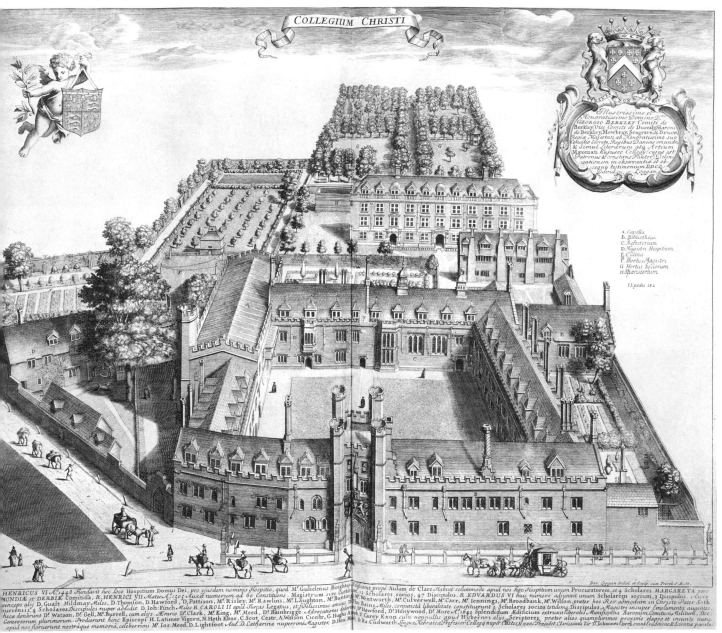

## 12. At Christ's: The Circle of Milton's Day

LIKE all his fellows, Milton was required to rise in time to be present at five-o'clock service of the Anglican Church, to which he was summoned by the bell of the college chapel. This was the custom, not only at Christ's, but throughout the university. Following an hour at service, the students gathered in the dining hall for breakfast. Then came lectures and examinations of the college tutors, with a tutor assigned to each student for his special guidance. In the latter part of the morning, each student was required to attend lectures or disputations in the "Public Schools" of the university, in which the student could hear renowned professors speak and advanced students from the various colleges engage in debate, the latter usually in Latin. At noon the students returned to Christ's College for dinner, after which they again heard disputations or orations by students of other colleges soon to graduate. The students were then free from college re-quirements for the day except for attendance at evening chapel service and supper at seven. Only in the afternoon and during and after supper were students allowed to lapse into conversational English; at other times they were expected to converse in Latin, Greek, or Hebrew. Nor were students allowed out in the evening, as Masson points out, "after nine o'clock from Michaelmas to Easter or . . . ten o'clock from Easter to Michaelmas." Many students escaped this restriction by climbing over the walls, despite sharp bits of glass embedded atop the masonry. They escaped also, despite strict penalties, to attend bearbaitings, cockfights, prize fights, dances, skittle-playings, Sturbridge Fair.

Such diversions held no charms for Milton, his mind now, whatever the disappointments in Cambridge in the years to follow, "all serious to learn and know." Later Milton was to be dubbed "the Lady of Christ's," less for his fair complexion than for his aversion to the unchaste habits of some of his fellow students. Even if Christianity had been "but slightly taught me," he was to

Reverendo admodum in Christo Patri ac Domino D^no THOMÆ BARLOW Lin- colniensi Episcopo, Collegii Regalis in Acad. CANTAB. juxta vim statutorū HENRICI 6^ti Regis et Fundatoris Illustrissimi (Ratione Episcopatus) pleno Jure VISITORI, Annum Octogessimum secundum, rite integritate, morumq suavitate, age- Ecclesiæ Anglicanæ Theologo nondum defatigato Fidei Orthodoxæ Patrono Summo, hanc Sacelli Delineationem a parte interiori accuratissimam tanquam Pietatis vere Regiæ r mentum, ad Futuram Tanti Viri, et Operis adeo augusti memoriam debita Reverentia D. D. C. Q. Dav: Loggan.

write in *An Apology*, "yet a certain reserv'dnesse of naturall disposition, and morall discipline learnt out of the noblest Philosophy was anough to keep me in disdain of farre lesse incontinences then this of the Burdello." When Charles Diodati wrote to Milton a year or so later, "I have no fault to find with my present mode of life, except that I am deprived of any mind fit to converse with. I long for such a person," he described Milton's own mood for a part of his Cambridge years. If the circle of the day was often barren in friendship with kindred spirits, Milton flew to his books and his dreams of a creative life to come.

## 13. Milton in the Public Schools

THOUGH by Milton's time instruction at Cambridge was centered in the various colleges under the direction of tutors, each student was required to spend a part of each day (usually late morning) attending university lectures at the Public Schools. Physically, the Public Schools consisted of a large building with a number of lecture halls, each accommodating students from the various colleges, who came to hear famed specialists in theology, logic, literature, philosophy, history, mathematics, rhetoric, and science. Such lectures were sponsored by the university government, not by the colleges. In addition, however, the Public Schools provided opportunities for the students to deliver orations, engage in debates, and become acquainted with brilliant young men among their contemporaries in other colleges. Milton's first Prolusion, "Whether Day or Night Is the More Excellent," was delivered at Christ's College; but his second, "On the Harmony of the Spheres," was delivered in the Public Schools, as well as Prolusion III, "An Attack on the Scholastic Philosophy." Of the seven academic exercises (all in Latin) which Milton himself preserved, four were delivered at Christ's College, three in the Public Schools. Such exercises were a means not only of testing himself but also of establishing his intellectual place among the most gifted young men of his Cambridge contemporaries.

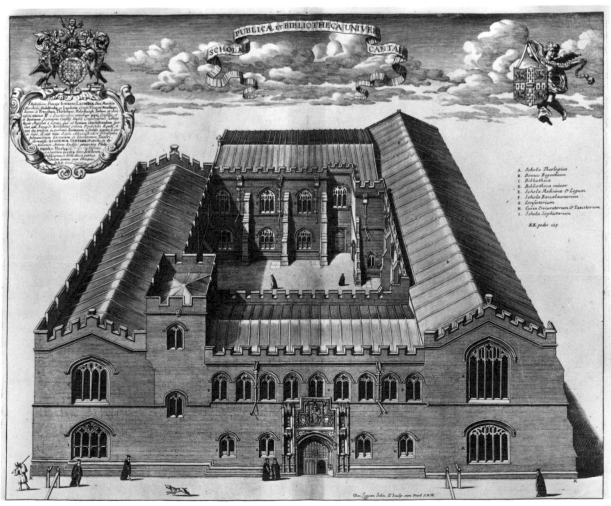

## 14. Milton and Diodati: Spring, 1626

IN THE spring of 1626 Milton was in difficulties with his tutor William Chappell, who, according to John Aubrey, "whip't him." Though it was very unusual for a tutor thus to punish a boy of seventeen (and Aubrey's story has never been authenticated), Milton's own words, "forbidden rooms," in a letter to Diodati, shows that the authorities of Christ's would not permit him (temporarily at least), to return to the college. But Milton was untroubled; he preferred London and his Bread Street home to Cambridge, especially when Diodati could be with him: "I refuse neither the name or the lot of the fugitive, and gladly I enjoy the condition of exile." He delighted in the theatre's many faces and dilemmas, humorous or sad. Moreover, in his leisure he gave himself up to the muses; "and books, which are my life, have me all to themselves."

How close Milton felt to Diodati appears in his comments about London girls who passed him on the streets. "Very often here," he wrote to Diodati, "as stars breathing forth mild flames, you may see troops of maidens passing by . . . . how often have I seen eyes surpassing all gems . . . and necks twice whiter than the arms of living Pelops . . . and the exquisite grace of the forehead; and the trembling hair which cheating Love spreads as his golden nets." These London girls, writes Milton, are more beautiful than the turbaned girls of Persia, the nymphs of Greece, or the young matrons of Troy. Such passages show how normally intense and electric was his response to the girls around him on London Streets. Some renowned critics maintain that Elegy 1 is only a conventional academic exercise, not a passionate utterance of his deep self, and this analysis cannot be disproved. Other scholars maintain that Milton is speaking to his closest friend from the depths of himself: writing with complete freedom and honesty on the delicate obsession that apparently pursued him daily in the spring of his seventeenth year.

## 15. Milton Defends His Manhood

IN THE summer or autumn of 1628, Milton was called upon to preside as "father" at the Vacation Exercise, a festive meeting in the hall of Christ's College: a time of frolic and rejoicing that the year's academic labors were over. Visitors from other colleges were present as well as fellows and students of Christ's. Milton called his audience "nearly the whole flower of the University." In this indirect praise of himself, as in later assertions of the high regard in which he was held by discriminating fellow students, Milton was astonishingly accurate. Yet he held himself aloof, and he had no sense of humor, though the occasion of the oration demanded it: "That Sportive Exercises on Occasion Are not Inconsistent with the Studies of Philosophy." In the prolusion that followed the Latin oration, Milton attempted some sallies of humor, scoffing at himself as the designated "father" of the occasion: "Why is it that *I* am so suddenly made Father? . . . Has some Thessalian witch smeared me with magic ointment?" Then Milton speaks (still in Latin) from a deep, resentful part of himself: "By some of you I used lately to be nicknamed 'The Lady.' Why seem I then too little of a man? . . . . Is it

14

because I never was able to quaff huge tankards lustily, or because my hands never grew hard by holding the plough, or because I never, like a seven years' herdsman, laid myself down and snored at midday; in fine, perchance, because I never proved my manhood in the same way as those debauched blackguards?" But Milton omitted the chief barbs of his detractors: he was called "The Lady of Christ's" more for his chastity than his fair skin and light brown hair.

15

## 16. Milton in Love

ON May 1, 1628, as he wrote in Elegy VII, Milton was walking along the streets of London, breathless again at the sight of so many beautiful girls, who at times seemed to him "a crowd of goddesses." On and on he walked, finally into the rural neighborhoods of London; as the morning advanced the sun shone "with two-fold brightness." Milton looked steadily into the eyes of lovely maidens along the way, but he was unable to stare them down. One girl especially made his heart race and throb: her mouth, her cheeks, even her eyebrows. "I inly burn," wrote Milton, "and am all one flame." But the beautiful one passed by, "snatched away . . . never to return." If only he could speak to her! She might not be made of stone; she might not be deaf to his pleas. In such a vein Milton opened his heart as he had done two years before to Diodati on the same theme. If Elegy VII is autobiographical (on which issue critics are divided), the Latin verses muted but did not conceal his desperation.

16

## 17. Street Cries of London

THOUGH Milton nowhere mentions the street cries of London, they could not have escaped his eyes or his ears as he walked around the Bread Street neighborhood, along the streets he knew so well. Pedlars were numerous on London streets: maidens carrying fresh cream and cheese on their heads, or carrots and cucumbers, or hot pudding pies, even hot eel pies; men with long brushes to sell, or hats and caps. A bearded man carrying an axe and hammer would cry, "Wood to cleave!" Then, after dark, the watchman with his spear, his lantern, his bell, and his dog. "Maids in your smocks," he would cry, "look well to your lock, your fire, and your light. And God give you good night!"

17

## 18. On the Morning of Christ's Nativity

WRITTEN only a few weeks after his twenty-first birthday, the Nativity Ode, a great poem by any mode of appraisal, marks the triumphant culmination of Milton's apprenticeship, a rise to the level of Spenser's art without as yet an exploration of the grandeur of blank verse. Rhyme to Milton was not as yet "a trivial thing, of no true musical delight." The thought of the poem is also conventional; the poet's anti-Trinitarian outlook is far, far off. The theological significance of Christmas (though not named as such) is explored in graceful imagery:

> The Babe lies yet in smiling infancy,
> That on the bitter cross
> Must redem our loss,
> So both himself and us to glorify;
> Yet first, to those ychained in sleep,
> The wakeful trump of doom must thunder
>     through the deep.

But the best passages of the Nativity are pale indeed beside the autobiographical passages of *Paradise Lost* or the depiction of the youth of Jesus in *Paradise Regained*.

The Shepheards. lu: 2.

8. And there were in the same countrey Shepheards abiding in y feild keeping watch ouer y flocke by night.
9. And loe y Angell of y Lord came vpon them etc.
16. And they came with hast and found Mary and Ioseph, and y babe lying in a manger.
20. And y shepheards returned glorifying and praysing God: etc.

## 19. The Plague in Cambridge: 1630

FROM April, 1630, to January, 1631, some 347 people in Cambridge died of the plague. Students and fellows fled homeward; the colleges were locked up, the streets deserted. Some 2800 citizens (who could not flee) were on public relief; these included many destitute people who served the colleges in menial positions. While most university officials and heads of colleges fled the infection, the Vice-Chancellor, Dr. Butts, remained at his post. About forty tents were set up on the commons to house the afflicted ones, who were ministered to by a German physician. "The late tempestuous rainy weather," wrote Dr. Butts, was thought to scatter the infection. The "disorderly poor" were dealt with promptly and severely. "Besides constables," wrote Dr. Butts, "we have certain ambulatory officers who walk the streets night and day, to keep our people from needless conversing." By royal proclamation the dioceses of London, Winchester, and Lincoln appealed for aid to the plague victims of Cambridge; some thousands of pounds were given to the cause. By October, 1630, the plague had "greatly abated," and the colleges were rapidly filling up again.

Dead.                Londons Charitie                Buried

the Conntries Crueltie

19

## 20. The Death of Hobson the Carrier

M.ʳ Hobſon          obyt anō 1630,
                    vixit annos 86.

DURING the plague months Hobson, the University carrier, was not permitted to make his weekly trips to London. He was a familiar and beloved figure in Cambridge, tough and agile, now in his eighty-sixth year. Some weeks before Christmas, though untouched by the plague, Hobson took to his bed, finally succumbing to death on New Year's Day, 1631. In his last weeks Hobson had added three codicils to his will, bequeathing the bulk of his property to six grandchildren and two surviving daughters (one of whom had married Sir Simon Clarke of Warwickshire). Hobson's will showed him to be a man of civic imagination as well as substance. He had bequeathed certain tenements to the town for the erection of a workhouse for the poor, these to be administered by twelve trustees, chosen equally from the town and the university. But Hobson's most imaginative bequest, as Masson points out, was "seven leys of pasture-land" for the maintenance in perpetuity of the conduit in the middle of the town, assuring a stream of fresh water coursing along Trumpington Street in all the years to come.

By the time of Hobson's death, or shortly after, Milton had probably returned to Christ's College. (It is certain that he was back by February 15, when his brother Christopher, age fifteen, was admitted to Christ's as lesser pensioner.) Hobson's death had put into focus his extraordinary qualities, but it did not move Milton to passionate utterance. He wrote two somewhat playful epitaphs about the carrier, both hobbled by rhymed couplets, neither of which may have satisfied the poet, though they later appeared in the 1645 edition of the poems. The word *superscription*, which ends the second epitaph, is one of the least poetic of words used in Milton's early poetry. The best lines are those of the first epitaph when Death, receiving Hobson,

> Showed him his room where he must lodge
> that night,
> Pulled off his boots, and took away the light.

## 21. Milton on Shakespeare: 1632

MILTON's poem, "An Epitaph on the Admirable Dramaticke Poet, W. Shakespeare," appeared anonymously in the Second Folio of 1632, along with laudatory verses by Ben Jonson, Leonard Digges, Hugh Holland, and others. Later, in the 1645 edition of the *Poems*, the Epitaph appeared as "On Shakespear. 1630." Written then in Milton's twenty-second year, his first to be published, the poem represents a passionate identification with creative values of a life in many ways alien to his own. How did Milton's admiration of Shakespeare grow? That it was not a new love is evident from the Epitaph. The First Folio had been accessible to him since his fifteenth year. Even before that he could not have been unaware of the Shakespearean performances at the Blackfriars, only a few minutes' walk from his Bread Street home; nor is there any evidence that Milton's father shared the Puritan dislike for the theatre. We recall the ecstatic passage to Diodati on the "resplendent theatre" of London, written by Milton in his eighteenth year. We cannot trace the steps by which Milton's love of Shakespeare deepened; but we cannot separate this devotion from Milton's growing ambition to become a great poet. In boyhood and youth the two men had been shaped from utterly dissimilar molds. Yet here is Milton crying "my Shakespeare," as if he had long cherished him in his heart's core. Milton could not have written these lines without immersing himself in the magic of Shakespeare's poetry and seeing the vast gulf that separated thus far his "slow-endeavouring art" from the master's flow of "easy numbers."

### An Epitaph on the admirable Dramaticke Poet, VV. SHAKESPEARE.

> WHat neede my Shakespeare for his honour'd bones,
> The labour of an Age in piled stones
> Or that his hallow'd Reliques should be hid
> Vnder a starre-ypointing Pyramid?
> Deare Sonne of Memory, great Heire of Fame,
> What needst thou such dull witnesse of thy Name?
> Thou in our wonder and astonishment
> Hast built thy selfe a lasting Monument:
> For whil'st to th'shame of slow-endevouring Art
> Thy easie numbers flow, and that each part,
> Hath from the leaves of thy unvalued Booke,
> Those Delphicke Lines with deepe Impression tooke
> Then thou our fancy of her selfe bereaving,
> Dost make us Marble with too much conceiving,
> And so Sepulcher'd in such pompe dost lie
> That Kings for such a Tombe would wish to die.

# The Years at Horton: 1632-1638

## 22. The *Commonplace Book*

AFTER receiving his M.A. and signing the graduation book (July 3, 1632), Milton began six years of fruitful leisure at his father's house, first at Hammersmith (until 1635), then at Horton, a village seventeen miles west of London and one mile from Colnbrook. Here Milton read "in the order of time," beginning with the Greek and Roman classics, digging deep into the church fathers, and so century by century up to his own age, unraveling the history and concepts of western Europe in chronological clarification. Although Milton had probably started the *Commonplace Book* in his Cambridge years, his most numerous notes were set down in 1636-1639 and 1640-1643. Fortunately the original volume of folio-sized leaves has survived intact. As James Holly Hanford has shown in "The Chronology of Milton's Private Studies," it illuminates as no other document Milton's gradual unfolding, individualizing his intellectual personality, now leaning toward Athens and the Renaissance, now toward Jerusalem. From some ninety authors Milton quotes passages favorable to divorce, polygamy, concubinage, organs, the theatre, plays; passages hostile to usury, lawyers, laws written in "Norman gibbrish," kingship, tyranny, courtiers, malign influence of the clergy on national policy.

23

## 23. *Arcades* at Harefield

POSSIBLY in late 1632 or the spring of 1633, Milton was asked to write the poetry for a masque at Harefield (eight or ten miles from Horton) in honor of the Countess Dowager of Derby, then in her early seventies. The request no doubt came from Henry Lawes, the court musician, who later produced *Comus* (and was probably known to Milton's father). Lawes was music tutor to the family of the Countess' stepson, the Earl of Bridgewater; it is likely that he composed the music for *Arcades*. On the appointed evening, the great mansion of the Countess (now no more, though the historic church where the Countess is entombed still stands nearby), was lighted up;

the Countess sat upon her throne, surrounded by older members of her family. The younger members of the family, dressed as Arcadian nymphs and carrying torches, advanced up the long avenue of elms known as "The Queen's Walk" (from the time of Queen Elizabeth's visit two and thirty years before). As they paused, a single voice sang out the first lines of Milton's verse:

> Look, Nymphs and Shepherds, look!
> What sudden blaze of majesty
> Is that which we from hence descry,
> Too divine to be mistook?

## 24. The Masque of *Comus*: September 29, 1634

FOLLOWING the success with *Arcades*, Milton was commissioned by Lawes to write the poetry for a masque at Ludlow Castle celebrating the inauguration of the Earl of Bridgewater as Lord President of the Council of Wales. Milton was free to select his own theme of chastity, a subject pervading his thoughts more intensely with each passing year: one that in a masque would require compelling arguments hostile as well as favorable to the concept. This theme was bone deep in Milton's broodings. It is likely that he was thinking also what he was to write three years later to Diodati, "You ask what I am meditating? By the help of Heaven, an immortality of fame. I am letting my wings grow and preparing to fly." In technical resources the poet was growing, too. In *Comus* for the first time he was to dispense in the main with rhyme. The internal music of the poetic line, the mingling of such consonants as *l*'s and *m*'s, loomed more vital to him as the years passed.

On the evening of September 29, the masque was presented probably in the great hall of Ludlow Castle, the walls of which are still standing. Lawes, who composed the music for the songs, himself took the role of the Attendant Spirit. The three children of the Earl of Bridgewater, Viscount Brackley, Thomas Egerton, and Lady Alice, acted the parts of the Elder and Second Brother and the Lady. Though the children were only eleven, nine, and fifteen years old, they had already acted in masques at court. Like other masques, *Comus* provided spectacle, singing, and

dancing. It also included, in the form of the character Comus and his beastly companions, a contrast to the graceful order and beauty of the performance as a whole. But Milton also expanded a serious and piercing theme in his masque, an element of unexpected depth and ordered beauty, set forth in poetic language no other contemporary had brought forth for such an occasion.

24A

24B

## 25. Death of Milton's Mother

SARAH MILTON died at Horton April 3, 1637. She was buried three days later under the floor of the chancel of Horton Church. The inscription on the flat blue stone, clearly visible to this day, is as follows: "Heare lyeth the body of Sara Milton, the wife of John Milton, who died the 3rd of April 1637." The mother of Milton was about sixty-five; she had borne her husband six children, of whom three had survived infancy: John, Anne, and Christopher. She had married her husband when she was about twenty-eight, he thirty-seven. Her eyes were weak, and she had worn glasses from the time she was about thirty, whereas her husband John was to read without glasses until the age of eighty. In his *Second Defence* Milton was to write, "My father was distinguished by the undeviating integrity of his life, my mother . . . by the alms which she bestowed." Undoubtedly Milton was a dutiful son to his mother as to his father; but if he wrote her letters of love and praise, as he did to his father, they have not been preserved.

## 26. The Sad Occasion of "Lycidas"

ON August 10, 1637, Edward King of Christ's College was on his way home to Ireland, sailing from Chester Bay along the northern coast of Wales. Suddenly the ship struck a rock and within a few minutes began to sink. Some passengers dived overboard and saved themselves by swimming and finally scrambling into one boat. Edward King made no attempt to save himself. He was last seen on his knees in prayer, and his body was not recovered.

When the students and fellows of Christ's College returned for the Michaelmas term, they resolved to publish a small volume of commemorative verses in honor of King, who had been at the college eleven years and was highly respected throughout the university community. Though his poetic talent was not remarkable, he had written a number of Latin poems in honor of the members of the royal family. As the volume for King crystallized in the autumn months, it contained two parts, separately paged: first, twenty-three contributions in Latin and Greek, called *Justa Edovardo King naufrago*; and second, thirteen poems in English, titled *Obsequies to the memorie of Mr Edward King*. Milton was either asked to contribute or volunteered his elegy, called "Lycidas," which appeared at the end of the English collection.

Milton was now twenty-nine. Though he considered himself still unready to write a great poem by his definition, his years of ripening at Horton had now borne fruit in a work of superlative creative power.

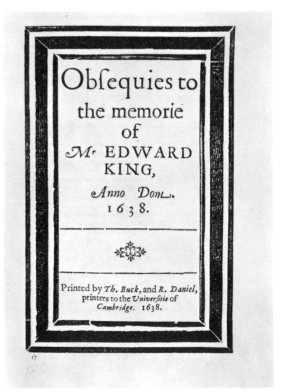

# Milton's Continental Tour: 1638-1639

## 27. With Grotius in Paris
### [late April or early May, 1638]

"I THEN became anxious to visit foreign parts," wrote Milton in *Second Defence*, "and particularly Italy. My father gave me his permission, and I left home with one servant. On my departure, the celebrated Henry Wotton, who had long been King James's ambassador at Venice, gave me a signal proof of his regard, in an elegant letter which he wrote [dated at Eton April 13, 1638], breathing not only the warmest friendship, but containing some maxims of conduct which I found very useful in my travels. The noble Thomas Scudamore, King Charles's ambassador, to whom I carried letters of recommendation, received me most courteously at Paris. His lordship gave me a card of introduction to the learned Hugo Grotius, at that time ambassador from the Queen of Sweden to the French court; whose acquaintance I anxiously desired, and to whose house I was accompanied by some of his lordship's friends." Phillips asserts that Grotius gave the young Englishman "entertainment suitable to his worth." That Milton continued to admire Grotius is evident from his reference to him in *Tetrachordon* as "yet living, and one of prime note among learned men." Milton's interest in

Grotius' *Christus Patiens* (in *Poemata Collecta*, Leyden, 1617) may be echoed in his use of the phrase "Christus patiens" in the Cambridge manuscript of possible ideas for tragedies. It is also likely that Milton knew Grotius' *Adamus Exul* (The Hague, 1601).

27A

27B

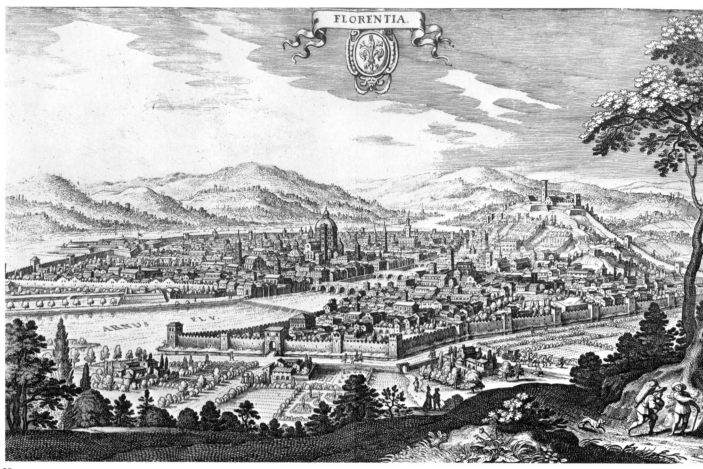

FLORENTIA.

ARNUS FLV.

28

29A

## 28. Milton Reaches Florence
### [by September 10, 1638]

AFTER spending only "a few days" in Paris, Milton travelled south through France at a leisurely pace. "Taking ship at Nice," he wrote later, "I arrived at Genoa, and afterwards visited Leghorn, Pisa, and Florence. In the latter city, which I have always more particularly esteemed for the elegance of its dialect, its genius, and its taste, I stopped about two months; when I contracted an intimacy with many persons of rank and learning; and was a constant attendant at their literary parties."

## 29. Friendships in Florence: The Academies

On September 16, 1638, within a week after his arrival in Florence, Milton read a Latin poem before the Svogliati Academy. From this time forth friendships between Milton and Florentine intellectuals blossomed and flourished. Milton wrote afterward: "No time will ever abolish the agreeable recollections which I cherish of Jacopo Gaddi, Carlo Dati, Frescobaldo, Coltellino, Bonmatthei, Clementillo, Francini, and many others." The Svogliati was only one of twenty such academies in Florence, some of which met at the various homes of their members, some in beautiful buildings of their own. About five hundred such academies throve in the Italy of Milton's time, distributed in 133 cities and towns: seventy in Bologna, fifty-six in Rome, forty-three in Venice, twenty-nine in Naples. In 1638 Renaissance zeal for such associations was nearly at its zenith. On September 10 Milton wrote a warm letter to Benedetto Bonmatthei, urging him to complete his work on the Italian language, and expressing his own delight in Dante and Petrarch. Was not the purity of the Greek tongue more than once the salvation of Athens? Milton reminded Bonmatthei of Plato's judgment that changes in habits of dress portend commotions in the commonwealth; but he, Milton, would rather judge that the fall of Athens followed the debasement of its speech. The great writers whom Bonmatthei celebrates, whether of tragedy, dialogues, or history, asserts Milton, have preserved the Florentine tongue in its purest form.

29B

ings of Fra Angelico or the cell of Savonarola in San Marco. What of Carlo Dati, then only nineteen, a member of many Florentine academies, already renowned and cherished for his remarkable oratory? Dati was an exceptionally fond and admiring friend to Milton, as shown by their correspondence over the years and the encomium which Milton preserved and later published in the 1645 *Poems*. No one would have been more eager than Dati to show Milton the glories of Florence. But we have no record of such an action, and Milton has left no visual record of the city he loved best, next to London.

## 30. What Did Milton See in Florence?

Milton does not mention the sculpture, the paintings, or even the architecture of Florence. He does not refer to the David of Michelangelo, or Ghiberti's bronze doors of the Baptistery in the heart of the city, which Michelangelo thought fit to adorn the gates of Paradise. Nor does Milton mention the font within the Baptistery, broken by Dante in a sudden dash to save a drowning child. Yet it cannot be imagined that in his two months in Florence one or several of Milton's eager friends did not take him to see Dante's house, or that of Guicciardini, the paint-

30

## 31. Milton Visits Galileo

IN *Areopagitica*, speaking of his visit to Florence, Milton wrote: "There it was that I found and visited the famous *Galileo* grown old, a prisner to the Inquisition, for thinking in Astronomy otherwise then the Franciscan and Dominican licencers thought." Now seventy-four, Galileo had become totally blind within the year past. In 1632 his *Dialogues concerning the Ptolemaic and Copernican Systems* had brought him a second summons to Rome and a prison sentence by the Inquisition. In 1633 he had been liberated from a Roman prison and permitted to return to Tuscany. Still under mild restrictions for his adherence to Copernican beliefs, Galileo lived in a villa at Arcetri, as Masson writes, on a "sunny

vine-clad slope, a little way out of Florence on the south side," with an old tower as his observatory. His telescopes he had constructed with his own hands. Galileo was scholar, musician, and poet as well as scientist. On occasion he would recite his own verses as well as passages from his favorite poet, Ariosto. In describing Satan's shield in *Paradise Lost* (I, 286-91), Milton refers again to Galileo:

> the broad circumference
> Hung on his shoulders like the moon, whose orb
> Through optic glass the Tuscan artist views
> At ev'ning from the top of Fesole,
> Or in Valdarno, to descry new lands,
> Rivers or mountains in her spotty globe.

31A

## 32. Milton in Rome

"FROM Florence," wrote Milton afterward, "I went to Siena, thence to Rome." Milton probably arrived in Rome near the end of September or in the early days of October; there he spent two months "viewing the antiquities of that renowned city." In these weeks Milton must have seen St. Peter's, designed in part by Michelangelo, only recently completed after the labors of 176 years; its architecture, critics have noticed, bears a rough resemblance to Milton's design of Pandemonium in Book II of *Paradise Lost*. Milton writes that in Rome he "experienced the most friendly attentions from Lukas Holsten, and other learned and ingenious men." Through Holsten, a German scholar of immense range (including three years at Oxford) and a protégé of Cardinal Francesco Barberini, Milton was able to examine in the Vatican, as he wrote to Holsten later, "many manuscript Greek authors set forth with your explanations," manuscripts that seemed to Milton to "demand the active hands of the printer, and a delivery into the world." Here was more excitement for Milton's Renaissance mind, one may guess, than Roman ruins and antiquities.

32A

32B

## 33. Milton and Roman Music: Leonora Baroni

WHILE in Rome Milton accepted an invitation to a musical concert at the Barberini Palace, where the great cardinal himself waited at the door to greet him. In Rome also Milton heard the matchless Leonora Baroni sing, perhaps accompanied (as often) by her mother on the theorbo and her sister on the harp. To hear Baroni was among the richest musical experiences the great city could provide. Milton was so moved that he wrote for Baroni three Latin epigrams, in one of which he compares her to Tasso's Leonora, "for the mad love of whom, he walked raging in the world."

## 34. In Naples: Milton and Manso

LEAVING Rome by coach and horse, probably in late November, 1638, Milton and his servant traveled south to Naples by easy stages. In the coach rode also "a certain eremite" whom Milton does not name. But the eremite spoke to him about the renowned Joannes Baptista Mansus, Marquis of Villa, "a most noble and important man," wrote Milton afterward, "to whom Torquatus Tasso, the famous Italian poet, addressed his Discourse on Friendship; and, as long as I stayed there, I experienced the most friendly attention from him, he himself acting as my guide through the different parts of the city . . . and coming himself, not once only, to my inn to visit me." Born in 1561, Manso was now seventy-seven; for over five decades he had been a generous and imaginative patron of the arts. From his twenty-eighth year Manso had befriended the great Tasso, then forty-four (born in 1544), who in his youth had been the idol of the court of Ferrara, renowned and gifted at nineteen. But in the last months of 1575, at thirty-one, a strange psychological illness gradually beset Tasso, accompanied by profound despair and threatened violence. In February, 1579, he was committed to prison, where he remained seven years. The fame of his *Aminta* (1573) and his *Gerusalemme Liberata* (1581) led to his release. He became an incessant wanderer, upheld by the care of friends who loved him and knew his need for quiet and solitude. Three times he came to stay at Manso's villa, where his spirit was at rest, his mind clear, his need for friendship fulfilled.

Milton's own gratitude to Manso he expressed in a Latin epistle, later published in the 1645 *Poems*, prefixed there by Tasso's lines of high tribute to Manso from his *Gerusalemme Conquistada*:

> Fra cavalier magnanimi, è cortesi
> Risplende il Manso.

34

## 35. Milton and Marini

I**N** HIS poetical tribute to Manso, Milton mentions the Neapolitan's friendship also for the poet Giambattista Marini (1569-1625). Upon his deathbed, wrote Milton, Marini "left his bones in trust" to Manso, who caused a bust of the poet to be erected in the Church of San Domenico Maggiore. Milton testifies in *Mansus* that he has seen the face of the poet "smiling down from his carved bronze," as indeed the visitor may see him to this day.

35

## 36. Milton and the Phlegraean Fields

MILTON's descriptions of Hell in Book 1 of *Paradise Lost* are the most vivid and realistic of the entire poem. It is entirely likely, as Marjorie Nicolson has shown in her "Milton's Hell and the Phlegraean Fields," that many of Milton's images came from a visit to the Fields, a few miles south of Naples, where the hot earth spouts streams of smoke and sulphur to this day. Then as now, new low craters in the Phlegraean Fields rose up overnight, belching sulphurous smoke and tiny rivers of hot sand.

## 37. Milton Retraces His Steps: A Second Visit to Florence

"WHEN I was preparing to pass over into Sicily and Greece [in December, 1638]," wrote Milton afterward, "the melancholy intelligence . . . of the civil commotions in England made me alter my purpose; for I thought it base to be travelling for amusement abroad, while my fellow-citizens were fighting for liberty at home." Turning northward, then, Milton spent about two months in Rome before going on to Florence (probably in early February, 1639), where he was received with enthusiasm by his friends of the academies, Dati, Gaddi, Frescobaldi, Bonmatthei, Coltellini, and all the others. Indeed his friends now made Florence seem almost a second home to him. The minutes of the Svogliati show that in March, 1639, Milton attended three of their meetings in succession. In the meeting of March 17 Milton and two others of the group read some "noble Latin verses." Milton again read Latin poems at the meeting of March 31. We know also that during his two months in Florence, Milton made a pilgrimage to Lucca, forty miles away, the original seat of the Diodati family.

From his vivid reference in *Paradise Lost* (1, 302-305), it is likely that Milton visited (on this stay or the one in autumn, 1638) the beautiful shady dale called Vallombrosa, its houses nestled on a steep slope of mountain side about eighteen miles from Florence:

> Thick as autumnal leaves that strow the brooks
> In Vallombrosa, where th' Etrurian shades
> High over-arched embow'r.

Reno River by ferry at Malalbergo. In the coach were several beautiful Italian girls and an "amorous youth." As they rode along, Milton's feelings for one of the girls welled forth in a "speech blossom" in her own tongue:

Thou graceful lady, whose fair name knows well
  The grassy vale through which the Reno strays,
  Nearing the noble ford, that man is base
  On whom thy gentle spirit exerts no spell,
That frankly makes its sweetness visible,
  At no time sparing of its winning ways,
  And of those gifts, Love's bow and piercing rays,
  Whereby thy lofty virtue doth excel.

Curious about the handsome young Englishman in their midst, the girls on the coach accosted Milton:

Laughing, the ladies and the amorous youth
Accost me round:- "Why dost thou write," ask they,
"Why dost thou write in foreign phrase and strain,
"Versing of love with daring so uncouth?
"Tell us; so may thy hope not be in vain,
"And thy best fancies have auspicious way!"

Some renowned Milton critics claim that these sonnets were written earlier than the Italian journey and not based on any personal experience in Italy. So far no hard proof has been brought forth for this analysis, but it cannot be disproved. The author prefers Masson's account to any other until more complete evidence is forthcoming.

## 38. To Bologna and Ferrara

"HAVING crossed the Apennines," wrote Milton, "I passed through Bologna and Ferrara on my way to Venice." Bologna upheld an ancient and flourishing intellectual tradition; its university was the oldest in Italy and its academies most prolific in number. At Ferrara Milton might have looked at the tomb of Ariosto and the prison in which Tasso lay in gloom for seven years. But Milton was more interested in people than in tombs or prisons, however profound his love of poets destined to earthly immortality. On the way by coach from Bologna to Ferrara, as Masson reconstructs his route, Milton crossed the

CANTO PRIMO
# MADRIGALI
## GVERRIERI, ET AMOROSI
Con alcuni opuſcoli in genere rappreſentatiuo, che ſaranno
per breui Epiſodij frà i canti ſenza geſto.
### LIBRO OTTAVO
## DI CLAVDIO MONTEVERDE
Maeſtro di Capella della Sereniſſima Republica di Venetia,
DEDICATI
### Alla Sacra Ceſarea Maeſtà
## DELL' IMPERATOR
# FERDINANDO III.
### CON PRIVILEGIO.

IN VENETIA,  A
Appreſſo Aleſſandro Vincenti. MDCXXXVIII.

39A

PIAZZA DE S. MARCO DI VENETIA.

39B

## 39. Milton in Venice

THOUGH Milton spent a full month in Venice, parts of April and May, 1639, we know less about his experiences there than at any large city of his tour. Edward Phillips writes that Milton shipped home from Venice "a chest or two of choice music-books of the best masters flourishing about that time in Italy,—namely, Luca Marenzo, Monte Verde, Horatio Vecchi, Cifra, the Prince of Venosa, and several others." But of the books on art or the art itself he must have seen "examining the city," not a word. If Milton stepped out of his gondola and visited the Scuola di San Rocco, its walls and ceiling aflame with Tintoretto's colors, he could not have turned away with indifference. And what of Titian? What of Jacopo Bellini and his sons Gentile and Giovanni?

## 40. Milton's Stay at Geneva: The Return to London

"AT GENEVA," wrote Milton in *Second Defence*, "I was daily in the society of John Diodati, the most learned Professor of Theology." Uncle of Charles Diodati (whose death in London Milton may now have heard about for the first time), Dr. Diodati was translator of the Bible and the leading Protestant intellectual in the Geneva community. Dr. Diodati lived in a great house "on the south bank of the lake, two miles out of the city, which has retained its name of the Villa Diodati to this day, and was tenanted in 1816 by Lord Byron." Through Diodati Milton met other refugee intellectuals, including Camillo Cerdogni's family. Like many visitors who had enjoyed Cerdogni hospitality, Milton wrote a passage in the family album:

— if Vertue feeble were
Heaven it selfe would stoop to her.
Coelum non animum muto dum trans mare curro.
Joannes Miltonius
Junii 10. 1639                   Anglus.

40A

From Geneva, then, turning homeward not earlier than the date of the lines from *Comus* in-
scribed in the Cerdogni album, Milton travelled
to Paris by way of Lyons and the Rhone Valley,
crossing to England in late July or early August,

1639. Proud of his unsullied chastity, assured
afresh of his flowering creative talent, he was
more certain than ever that his quest for an "immortality of fame" was within the reach of his
eager mind and lofty purpose.

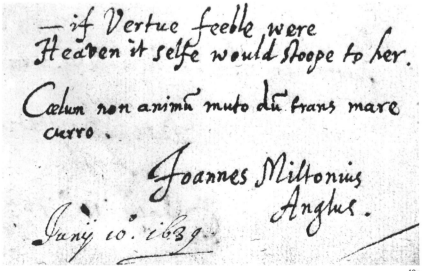

40B

## 41. Schoolmaster at St. Bride's Churchyard

UPON his return to England, after visiting his father and seeing old friends, Milton rented a lodging in St. Bride's Churchyard and became tutor of his two nephews, Edward and John Phillips, then nine and ten years old, sons of his dead sister Anne. Milton was their tutor some five years. For a while they were joined by the young lad Sir Thomas Gardiner, sent to Milton by his friend Lady Ranelagh; from time to time other sons of friends came under Milton's tutelage, which is described with high praise in Edward Phillips' biography of his uncle: "Neither his Converse, nor his Writings, nor his manner of Teaching ever savour'd in the least any thing of Pedantry." The classics included Pliny, Vitruvius, Cato, Varro, Lucretius, Hesiod, Aratus, Xenophon. The first works studied, according to Aubrey, were Cato, Varro, and the *De Re Rustica* of Lucius Columella. Every Sunday the boys read a chapter in Greek from the New Testament. Though strict, even severe, as a teacher, Milton was "familiar and free in his conversation." Music was a part of the daily lessons: "He made his Nephews Songsters," writes Aubrey, "and sing from the time they were with him."

41

Baynards Castle

# Milton as Revolutionary:
## Prelude to Civil War

### 42. Milton against the Prelates

IN THE months that followed his return to England, Milton had drawn up some ninety-nine possible topics for a tragedy, about two-thirds of them Scriptural and one-third historical. But the agitation against Bishop Hall's *Episcopacy by Divine Right* (April, 1640) and the fiery debates that accompanied the meeting of the Long Parliament (November, 1640) injected Milton into a political struggle that in him was bone-deep: a struggle that was to bring Charles I to the block and continue for twenty years, meanwhile destroying kingship and sending twenty thousand more Englishmen to sanctuary in the wilds of America. "The vigour of the Parliament," wrote Milton afterward, "had begun to humble the pride of the bishops. As long as the liberty of speech was no longer subject to control, all mouths began to be opened against the bishops. . . . I saw that a way was opening for the establishment of real liberty; that the foundation was laying for the deliverance of man from the yoke of slavery and superstition . . . and as I had from my youth studied the distinctions between religious and civil rights, I perceived that if I ever wished to be of use, I ought at least not to be wanting to my country, to the Church, and to so many of my fellow-Christians, in a crisis of so much danger." To engage in this struggle, Milton unhesitatingly deferred the realization of his great dream, to "leave something so written to aftertimes, as they should not willingly let it die." Within a year (May, 1641, to April, 1642), Milton wrote five pamphlets that embodied his main ideas of civil reform: *Of Reformation, Of Prelatical Episcopacy, Animadversions, Reason of Church-Government*, and *An Apology against a Pamphlet*. In composing these pamphlets, Milton was aware that his style often lacked grace and distinction. In the craft of prose writing, he wrote, "I have the use, as I may account it, but of my left hand."

42

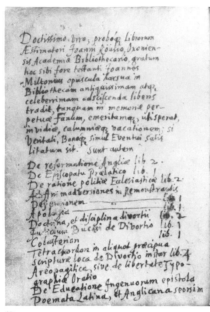

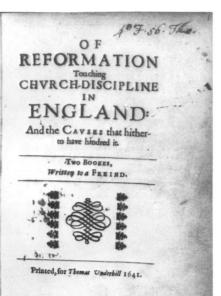

D. IOHANNES ROVSE A.M. PROTOBIBLIOTHECARIVS ELECTVS MENSE MAIO MDCXX, OBIIT MENSE APRILE MDCLII.

43A

43B

## 43. Milton and John Rous

IN 1635, when Milton was incorporated Master of Arts at Oxford (and an equivalent number of Oxford men were incorporated M.A. at Cambridge), it is likely that he met for the first time John Rous, chief librarian of the Bodleian. The two men became friends. When the Civil War broke out, Rous was sympathetic to Parliament's cause. Some years later, when Milton had written some eleven pamphlets in all, he presented to the Bodleian at Rous's suggestion a collection of these pamphlets bound together (in order of publication) as well as a copy of his 1645 *Poems*. On a blank page at the beginning of the volume, Milton had written the titles of his eleven prose works already published, together with the Latinized title of the 1645 *Poems*.

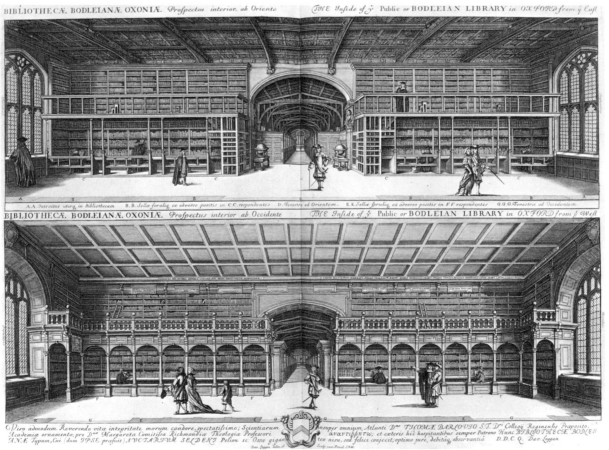

43C

## 44. Puritan Leaders Granted Liberty

ONE of the first actions of the Long Parliament was to release from prison three zealous and distinguished opponents of the bishops: John Bastwick, a physician, William Prynne, a lawyer, and Henry Burton, a minister; all three had suffered close imprisonment in the Channel and Scilly Islands since 1637. The Star Chamber had sentenced each to have his ears cut off in the pillory (a second such mutilation for Prynne), to forfeit his professional credentials, and to be denied visitation in jail by his wife and children. On November 7, 1640, the House ordered that the three agitators be released to appear before the Commons. On November 28 Prynne and Burton entered London in a blaze of triumph, amid the cheers of many thousands; on December 4 the tumultuous citizens met and surrounded Bastwick with joyous acclamation.

M: Henry Burton, for preaching againſt Popiſh innovations and printing his 2 Sermons For God & the King, was much vexed in the high Commiſſion Court, afterward cenſured in the Starr-Chamber to be deprived of his Miniſtrie, degraded in the Vniverſty, loſt both his Eares on the pillorie, was fined 5000.# baniſhed into the Ile of Gernſey, there Comitted to perpetuall cloſs impriſonment, where no freinds, no not ſo much as his wife or Children might once ſee or come into the Iſland where hee was on pain of impriſonment to them. Which Corporall puniſhment was Executed on him, and his two other bleſſed Brethren or fellow-Sufferers, June 30ᵗʰ 1637.

44B

Dᴿ Baſtwick, for writing a Booke againſt Popiſh-Biſhops was firſt fined 1000.# and Committed Cloſs-priſoner in the Gatehouſe, by the high Commiſſion. After that for writing of the Parity of Miniſters, &c. was cenſured in the Starr-Chamber to be deprived of his practiſe in Phyſick, to looſe both his Eares in the pillorie, was fined 5000.# baniſhed into the Iſle of Sillyes and there Committed to perpetuall cloſs impriſonment, where hee was moſt cruelly uſed, and no freinds, no not ſo much as his wife or Children once permitted to ſee him on pain of impriſonment as afore ſaid.

W. Hollar fecit

44A

Mr: William Prynne, for writing a booke againſt Stage-players called Hiſtrio-maſtix was firſt cenſured in the Starr-Chamber to looſe both his Eares in the pillorie, fined 5000.# & perpetuall impriſonment in the Towre of London. After this, on a meer ſuſpition of writing other bookes, but nothing at all proved againſt him, hee was again cenſured in the Starr-chamber to looſe the ſmall remainder of both his eares in the pillorie, to be Stigmatized on both his Cheekes with a firey-iron, was fined again 5000.# and baniſhed into yᵉ Iſle of Ierſey, there to ſuffer perpetuall-Cloſs- impriſonmᵗ: no freinds being permitted to ſee him, on pain of impriſonment

44C

Gaze not upon this shaddow that is vaine,
But rather raise thy thoughts a higher straine,
To GOD (I meane) who set this young-man free,
And in like straits can eke deliuer thee.

45

## 45. Cromwell's Speech for Lilburne

ON November 7 Oliver Cromwell rose in the Commons to speak for John Lilburne, an obscure agitator, no university man like Prynne or Bastwick. Cromwell was now forty-one, a prosperous gentleman farmer, cousin to John Hampden (and related to eighteen other members of the Commons). In his boyhood and youth, including a year at Sidney Sussex College, he had excelled in cudgels and football; his wrestling with ideas had been weak and ineffectual. Though one member, Warwick, was amazed that Cromwell now spoke with such fervor about the fate of an unknown disperser of pamphlets (as if the government itself were in danger), he could see that the House gave him close attention:

> His linen was plain, and not very clean; and I remember a speck or two of blood upon his little band, which was not much larger than his collar; his hatt was without a hattband: his stature was of a good size, his sword stuck close to his side, his countenance swoln and reddish, his voice sharp and untunable, and his eloquence full of fervor . . . but the subject matter would not bear much of reason.

46

## 46. John Lilburne Whipped in Fleet Street

LILBURNE, apprentice rebel, had been accused by Laud as "one of the notoriousest disperser[s] of Libellous *bookes* . . . in the Kingdome." On January 14, 1637, Lilburne had been committed to the Gatehouse for transporting scandalous books from Holland to England. After refusing repeatedly to take the Star Chamber oath "to answer in truthful terms," Lilburne had been lashed through the streets (April 18, 1638) from the Fleet to Westminster, suffering two hundred strokes of a corded whip. According to Lilburne's account, he won even the executioner's admiration: "I have whipt many a Rogue, but now I shall whip an honest man, but be not discouraged . . . it will be soone over." Required to stand in the pillory, Lilburne distributed Bastwick's pamphlets to the many sympathizers who surrounded him, saying, "There is part of the Bookes for which I suffer . . . I am stung by the *Scorpions* (the *Prelates*)." In Lilburne's humorless fanaticism loomed a portent of England's ills to come. If no one stood by him, declared Lilburne, friend, or wife, or child, he would "entertain Christ naked and alone."

## 47. Unanimous Proceedings against Laud

ON February 24, 1641, John Pym made a long speech in the Commons against Archbishop Laud, charging him with high treason, whereupon the Commons voted unanimously for the articles of impeachment. Two days later, on the 26th, Pym, Hampden, and Maynard carried the impeachment papers to the House of Lords, where Pym read them and urged their immediate adoption. Some men, asserted Pym, "set up the King above the Laws of the Kingdom"; yet in matters ecclesiastical they "endeavour to set up themselves above the King." The Lords ordered that Laud be removed to the Tower on the following Monday, March 1. At the appointed time, as Laud was passing through the streets, a mob of apprentices surrounded his carriage, shouting violent threats and epithets, harassing him to the very gates of the Tower, "even beyond," wrote Laud afterward, "*Barbarity* it self." Though the fatal stroke was nearly four years away, Laud was already a doomed man. Thus far Lords and Commons were united against excesses of arbitrary ecclesiastical power, the right arm of the monarch; doubts and divisions were yet to come.

## 48. The Bishops under Fire

ON March 10 the Commons called for a bill that would void both the bishops' legislative and judicial functions in the House of Lords. Next day, March 11, the Commons took a much more decisive step, calling for a bill that would void the bishops' sitting in the Star Chamber or any other court of civil law as an impediment "to ther spirituall function, prejudiciall to the Commonwealth." But to many members of the Commons such steps were not enough; already they wanted the elimination of all twenty-five bishops, the "root and branch" annihilation of their ecclesiastical as well as secular offices. Satire against the prelates, not merely against their courts (which sentenced men to prison and torture), mounted apace in the pamphlet magic hawked daily on the streets of London. Milton's own pamphlets of 1641-1642 were a learned and often bitter element in this stream of propaganda.

49A

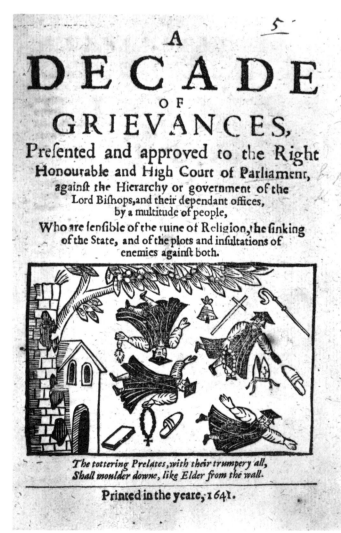

## 49. The Fall of Strafford

TO THE businessmen of London, as well as to the gentry and aristocracy of the Commons, Strafford was a symbol of the struggle for power between Charles and his Parliament. If Parliament could put Strafford to death, men's purses would be safe from the arbitrary hands of the king's officers, successors to the hated earl. In late April, 1641, when it became evident that Parliament could only doubtfully justify the charge of treason against Strafford, the Commons substituted a bill of attainder. On April 28 the Commons expressed a fear that Strafford would attempt an escape from the Tower. A few days later a plot was revealed to admit a hundred armed men into the Tower upon the king's order. Tumultuous crowds now surrounded the Houses daily, demanding the head of Strafford. On May 3 a mob of shopkeepers and merchants appeared at the Lords, shouting for justice against Strafford and holding up a placard displaying fifty-nine names of Commons members who had resisted passage of the bill of attainder. On May 5, when Pym declared that a plot was under way to overawe Parliament with a show of military force, the last doubts of reluctant members were dissolved. Mounting pressure for the Lords' concurrence with Strafford's fate could no longer be denied. In a singularly chivalrous letter (revealing a mind traced deep with feudal patterns), Strafford requested Charles to pass the bill "for prevention of Evils which may happen by your Refusal, to pass this BILL." After a long conference with his chaplains on May 10, Charles signed the fatal document. Unlike Cromwell and Strafford, the king was not a man of action in decisive moments. This weakness in Charles made royal dictatorship impossible in 1641 and prepared the way for the Puritan Revolution to follow.

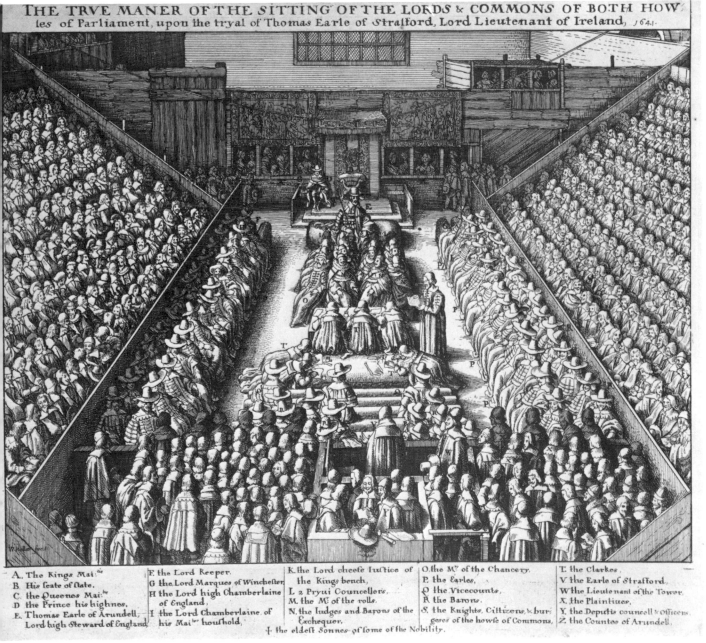

THE TRVE MANER OF THE SITTING OF THE LORDS & COMMONS OF BOTH HOWſes of Parliament, upon the tryal of Thomas Earle of Strafford, Lord Lieutenant of Ireland, 1641.

A. The Kings Ma.tie
B. His ſeate of ſtate.
C. the Queenes Ma.tie
D. the Prince his highnes.
E. Thomas Earle of Arundell, Lord high Steward of England.
F. the Lord Keeper.
G. the Lord Marques of Wincheſter
H. the Lord high Chamberlaine of England,
I. the Lord Chamberlaine of his Maiſter houſhold,
K. the Lord cheefe Iuſtice of the Kings bench,
L. 2 Pryui Councellors,
M. the Mr of the rolls,
N. the Iudges and Barons of the Exchequer,
† the eldeſt Sonnes of ſome of the Nobility.
O. the Mr of the Chancery.
P. the Earles,
Q. the Vicecounts,
R. the Barons,
S. the Knights, Cittizens, & burgeses of the howſe of Commons,
T. the Clarkes,
V. the Earle of Strafford,
W. the Lieutenant of the Tower,
X. the Plaintiues,
Y. the Deputis councell & Officers,
Z. the Countes of Arundell,

## 50. Strafford on the Scaffold

ON May 12 Strafford, dressed in black and carrying white gloves, walked through crowds of hushed spectators to the gibbet on Tower Hill. At forty-nine his tall frame was a little stooped, his black hair streaked with gray. Ascending the scaffold, he spoke to his friends, among them Bishop Ussher, the Earl of Cleveland, and his brother George Wentworth. To the king's majesty, said Strafford, he died loyal, grateful that Charles did not think him deserving of his penalty. Strafford denied that he had ever been opposed to Parliaments; they were indeed the "happy Constitution of the Nation." After his speech Strafford continued the ritual of execution: he removed his doublet, wound up his hair, put on a white cap, knelt to pray, and twice tested his head upon the block. Finally he stretched out his arms to signal the executioner, who struck off his head in one blow.

To Milton the punishment of Strafford was just and exemplary. In *Eikonoklastes* he was to call it "the most seasonable and solemn peece of Justice, that had bin don of many yeares in the Land." Indeed, declared Milton, in a passage singularly unfair, Strafford had no friends except the worst courtiers and clergymen of his time.

## 51. Abortive Arrest of the Five Members

BY THE first days of 1642 profound distrust between Charles and the Commons' majority needed only a spark to ignite the explosion of civil war. When Charles received the report that the Pym faction was preparing to impeach Queen Henrietta Maria (against whom evidence was more damning than against Laud or Strafford), his reliance on constitutional resistance instantly dissolved. The danger to the Queen was too great to permit even an hour's delay. On the morning of January 3, Attorney General Herbert appeared at the doors of the Lords with seven articles of impeachment against Pym, Hampden,

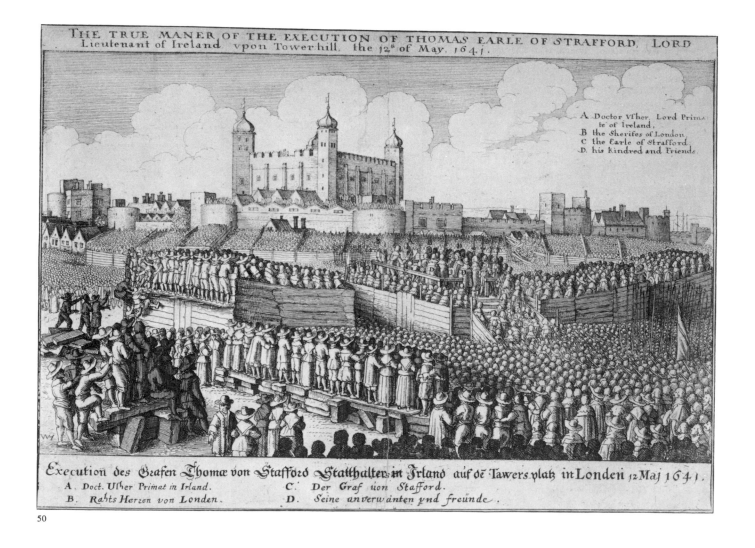

THE TRUE MANER OF THE EXECUTION OF THOMAS EARLE OF STRAFFORD, LORD Lieutenant of Ireland, vpon Tower-hill, the 12ᵗʰ of May, 1641.

A. Doctor Vſher, Lord Primate of Ireland.
B. the Sherifes of London.
C. the Earle of Strafford.
D. his kindred and Friends.

Execution des Grafen Thomæ von Stafford Statthalter in Irland auf dē Tawers platz in London 12 Maj 1641.
A. Doct. Uſher Primat in Irland.    C.   Der Graf von Stafford.
B.  Rahts Herzen von London.    D.   Seine anverwánten ynd freúnde.

Haselrig, Hollis, and Strode. The Lords did not act; they considered it their responsibility to impeach, not the monarch's. When the king's Sergeant at Arms Francis appeared at the Commons to arrest the five members, he was turned away with the message that the House would return a reply by one of its own members.

On the afternoon of January 4, having rashly resolved to arrest the five members in person, Charles approached the House between lanes of armed guards. Meanwhile the five members, by order of the House, had left their places and departed in order "to avoid Combustion in the House, if the said Soldiers should use Violence." Charles entered the House and walked toward the Speaker's chair. Finally he spoke to Lenthall, saying, "*By your Leave, (Mr. Speaker) I must borrow your Chair a little.*" Charles looked around in vain for the five absent members. Then he spoke to the House in part as follows:

> I Am sorry for this occasion of comming unto you: yesterday I sent a Sergeant at Arms upon a very important occasion, to apprehend some that by my command were accused of high Treason, whereunto I did expect Obedience, and not a Message.

51A

After this confrontation, no man in London would venture to arrest the five members for the king. The great city was a hotbed of resistance. Charles afterward regretted in *Eikon Basilike* (or Gauden for him) that he had not called the Parliament to meet in any city of England other than London. On January 12, having left the metropolis, Charles announced that he would abandon legal impeachment of the five members, asserting that he would take action against them in a way not to be challenged.

51B

The dolefull Lamentation of
Cheap-fide Croffe:
Or old England fick of the Staggers.

*The diffenting, and difagreeing in matters of opinion, together
with the fundry forts of Sects now raving and reigning, being the maine caufes of the difturbance and hinde-
rance of the Common-wealth.*

London. Printed for *F. C.* and *T. B.* 1641.

52A

52B

## 52. The Cross at Cheapside: Target of Fanaticism

ON January 24, 1642, the cross at Cheapside, only a few minutes' walk from Milton's birthplace, was set upon by a mob of sectarians and broken to pieces. In the flurry of pamphlets that followed this action, one of the most revealing was *The Dolefull Lamentation of Cheapside Cross*. The Cross deplores the proliferation of sects to whom surplices "are Smocks of the whore of *Rome*" and every thing "contrary to their opinion, is by them accounted profane." And who are these fanatics? "None but sanctified & shuttleheaded Weavers," answers the Cross, "long-winded Box-makers . . . thumping Felt-makers . . . and round-headed Button makers, which spoyle Bibles, while they thumbe over the leaves with their greasie fingers." Their zeal seethes and boils in absurd scriptural interpretations, communicated to loving as well as believing sisters. The world is "so mad with a supposition of knowledge, that whereas heretofore there was the Priests and the people, now the common people will be Priests." What is the root of such madness? Is it the "new wine lately come from *New-England*"? Thus Jasper Cross: and such strange notions in religion would soon lead to secular heresies as well.

## 53. Flight of the Great Seal

BY March 19 Charles had established himself at York, two hundred miles north of London, expecting those loyal to him to follow, and asserting exclusive command of the various county militias. Meanwhile the Great Seal remained in the hands of Lord Keeper Edward Lyttleton. On May 21 Lyttleton fled secretly from London toward York, after sending the Great Seal ahead of him by dependable hands. For a king's man to stay in London was now fraught with danger: Edward Hyde had secretly preceded Lyttleton to reach his royal master. When it became known that the Great Seal had been spirited away and the Lord Keeper no longer occupied the wool-sack in the House of Lords, a pall of consternation spread over London. The magic symbol of national unity and common purpose, reaching back through the centuries, was now no more.

53

## 54. A Divided Nation: the Drift Toward War

CHARLES'S withdrawal to York, thence to Oxford, forced men to choose sides. In the House of Lords the absentees on April 21, 1642, numbered sixty-one; but before the end of May, after the Lord Keeper's flight to Charles, eighty-two peers were absent, leaving only forty-two in attendance out of a possible 124. The Long Parliament had begun its work with 150 peers summoned by Charles, including twenty-six spiritual peers (twenty-four bishops and two archbishops) later banished from the Lords. Month by month, in the summer of 1642, the number of Lords in attendance dwindled still further, no more than thirty of them in steady attendance. In the House of Commons, which had begun with five hundred members, daily attendance now shrank to two hundred. The House decreed that all members not in their places on June 16 should be fined a hundred pounds each. On that day forty-five members were absent, presumably to join the king, among them Falkland, Hyde, Colepepper, Philip Warwick, John Ashburnham, and Sir Ralph Hopton. There was a much larger House than usual that day, however, under threat of the fine imposed, with three divisions, as Masson points out, of 142-122, 147-91, and 100-79. As the House was divided, so was the nation, with many brave men, though still in doubt, riding to join the banners of the king. By August 22, when Charles, moving south from York into the heart of England, set up his standard at Nottingham, there was no turning back.

54

## 55. The Opposing Armies: Courage and Fanaticism

By October, 1642, the royalist forces could muster 40,000 soldiers, 25,000 horse and 15,000 foot. On Parliament's side the forces numbered 25,000 foot and 5,000 horse, the latter divided into about seventy-five troops, each with sixty mounted men. Cromwell organized a troop of soldiers from the countryside around Huntingdon (supplying them largely from his own funds); twelve other members of the Commons served, like Cromwell, as captains of troop volunteers. But Cromwell's men, freeholders and sons of freeholders, were highly religious, dedicated spirits. After early defeats suffered by Parliament, Cromwell said to Hampden, "You must get men of a *spirit* . . . of a spirit that is likely to go on as far as gentlemen will go: or else you will be beaten still." Against the great tradition of aristocratic courage, reaching back through the centuries, Cromwell posed, then, the fanaticism of the Puritan believer.

55A

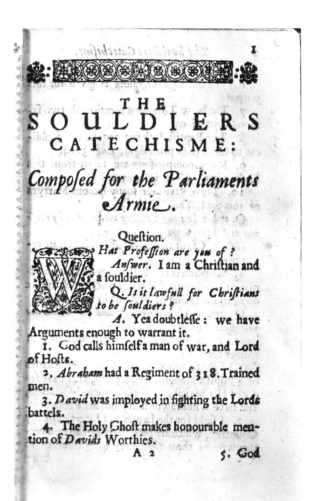

87.

# THE SOULDIERS CATECHISME:

Composed for

*The Parliaments Army:*

Confifting of two Parts : wherein are chiefly taught :

1 *The Iuftification* } of our Souldiers.
2 *The Qualifications*

Written for the Incouragement and Inftruction of all that have taken up Armes in this Caufe of God and his People; efpecially the common Souldiers.

2 Sam. 10.12. *Be of good courage, and let us play the men for our people, and for the Cities of our God, and the Lord do that which feemeth him good.*

Deut. 23.9. *When the Hoft goeth forth againft thine enemies, then keepe thee from every wicked thing.*

Imprimatur. JA. CRANFORD.

*Aprill: 8th*
Printed for J. Wright in the Old-Baily. 1644.

55B

1

*The Souldiers Catechifme.*

# THE SOULDIERS CATECHISME:

*Compofed for the Parliaments Armie.*

Queftion.

**W**Hat Profeffion are you of ?
  Anfwer. I am a Chriftian and a fouldier.
  Q. *Is it lawfull for Chriftians to be fouldiers ?*
  A. Yea doubtleffe : we have Arguments enough to warrant it.
  1. God calls himfelf a man of war, and Lord of Hofts.
  2. *Abraham* had a Regiment of 318. Trained men.
  3. *David* was imployed in fighting the Lords battels.
  4. The Holy Ghoft makes honourable mention of *Davids* Worthies.
                    A 2                      5. God

55C

## 56. The Death of Falkland

ON THE morning of the battle of Newbury, September 20, 1643, Lucius Carey, Viscount Falkland, thirty-three years old, dressed himself in clean linen. To his comrades he was gravely joyful, certain that his time had come. He could no longer bear the sadness of brave Englishmen slaughtering each other. Weary of the insoluble dilemmas of the conflict, Falkland told his comrades that he would be "out of it ere night." Mounting his horse when the battle began, the young man placed himself as a volunteer under Sir John Byron. Seeing a gap in the hedge through which bullets were whistling, Falkland spurred his charger through the opening and was shot down; he died instantaneously. By common consent of his great contemporaries, Puritan or Cavalier, Falkland was the flower of English chivalry. Living at Great Tew, only seventeen miles from Oxford, he attracted thither the choice spirits of his age, "men of the most eminent and sublime partes," wrote Clarendon, "and of untouched reputations in pointe of integrity: and such men had a title to his bosome." His very house, in Clarendon's view, "was a University bounde in a lesser volume."

## 57. Why Did Milton Not Enlist?

IT IS certain that Milton aspired to become a soldier in the Parliamentary army, to fight for a cause he believed in with religious passion. In 1639 he had cut short his tour to engage in the political struggle at home. "When I was preparing to pass over into Sicily and Greece," he wrote, "the melancholy intelligence which I received of the civil commotions in England made me alter my purpose; for I thought it base to be travelling for amusement abroad, while my fel-

56

low-citizens were fighting for liberty at home." Milton habitually wore a sword and practiced with it daily; he thought of himself as a match for any man, though taller and heavier than he. In 1642 Londoners practiced military drill daily on the City Artillery Ground near Milton's house. It is likely that Milton participated in these drills; it is clear that he knew the pike manual, company drill and battalion drill. Moreover, Milton was a man, in Cromwell's phrase, "of a spirit," as shown later by sending forth the second edition of *The Readie & Easie Way* in April, 1660, at the risk of his life. But in 1642, beset by ambivalent feelings, Milton decided, as he wrote afterward in *Second Defence*, that while "fighting men should do such illustrious actions, there were yet others" by whom God wished "these actions should be expounded and set forth . . . and the truth so defended by arms defended also by reason." Any soldier of greater strength, Milton felt, might easily have surpassed his own usefulness on the battlefield; his contribution should be of a different kind and no less vital to his country's cause.

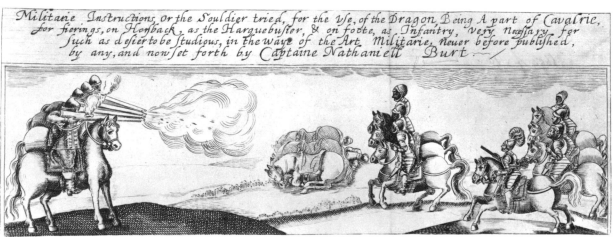

58A

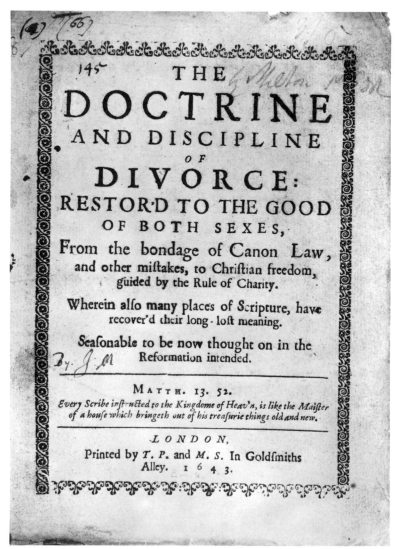

# THE
# DOCTRINE
## AND DISCIPLINE
### OF
# DIVORCE:
## RESTOR'D TO THE GOOD
### OF BOTH SEXES,

From the bondage of Canon Law,
and other miſtakes, to Chriſtian freedom,
guided by the Rule of Charity.

Wherein alſo many places of Scripture, have
recover'd their long-loſt meaning.

Seaſonable to be now thought on in the
Reformation intended.

MATTH. 13. 52.

*Every Scribe inſtructed to the Kingdome of Heav'n, is like the Maiſter
of a houſe which bringeth out of his treaſurie things old and new.*

LONDON,
Printed by *T. P.* and *M. S.* In Goldſmiths
Alley. 1 6 4 3.

58B

## 58. Milton's Sudden Marriage

ABOUT Whitsunday, May 21, 1642, Milton left his home on Aldersgate Street, travelled to Oxford, then the king's headquarters, and made his way to the Forest Hill home of Richard Powell, a few miles from the center of the city. Despite Mr. Powell's loyalty to Charles's cause, Milton was well received by the family, paid court to the daughter Mary, then seventeen, and within a month returned with her to London, a married man, accompanied also by several relatives of the bride. Accustomed to merriment and dancing in the great house at Forest Hill, Mary Powell soon found her life solitary, and in July asked permission to return for a visit to Forest Hill. But a deeper reason for the wife's departure (and failure to return at the appointed time), appears in Milton's *Doctrine and Discipline of Divorce*, in which Milton bemoans not only the lack of a "meet and happy conversation" but also the obstacle of "a body impenetrable." If this phrase means (which some eminent scholars doubt), that Mary Powell refused Milton the marriage act, there could have been no greater humiliation to him than this. When his wife did not return as promised by September 29, Milton was already considering the imperious need for divorce not only in a life as upright as his own but also in the lives of any of his countrymen deprived of a true marriage.

## 59. Reconciliation with Mary Powell: Later Marriages

IN July or August, 1645 (when the Civil War was turning against the royalists), Milton was reconciled to Mary Powell, who bore him four children: Anne, Mary, John (who died in infancy), and Deborah. About three days after the birth of Deborah, May 2, 1652, Mary Powell died. On November 12, 1656, Milton (now blind for several years) married Katherine Woodcock, who died on February 3, 1658, six weeks before the death of an infant daughter. Of Katherine, Milton wrote the sonnet beginning, "Methought I saw my late espousèd saint." Five years later Milton married Elizabeth Minshull, who outlived her husband some fifty-three years. It is clear from Milton's Latin treatise *Christian Doctrine* (not discovered until 1825), that he was guilty of a far more fundamental heresy than that of divorce. He believed also in polygamy, in justification of which he cites examples of Biblical heroes and prophets.

## 60. Milton Among the Heretics

ON August 13, 1644, about one year after the appearance of *Doctrine and Discipline of Divorce* and four weeks after *The Judgement of Martin Bucer Concerning Divorce*, Herbert Palmer, in a sermon to the Parliament, called attention to Milton's divorce heresy, toleration of which would be unthinkable: "*of which a wicked book is abroad and uncensured, though deserving to be burnt.*" Moreover, the author had signed his name and dedicated it to Parliament! To the heretical opinions abroad in the land, such as those of the Jesuits, the Arminians, the Anabaptists, the Seekers, the Familists, was now added that of the Divorcer.

## 61. Comenius in England

AFTER ten years of encouraging correspondence with his friend Samuel Hartlib, the renowned Moravian educator John Amos Comenius arrived in London, September 21, 1641. Comenius was possessed by a great dream: free public schools in every community which all boys and girls, rich or poor, could attend. On the verge of revolution, would England listen to the most crucial reform of all? Samuel Hartlib had high hopes for his friend's leading principles, which he had caused to be translated and published as *Reformation of Schooles* (with an outline of *The Great Didactic* to come); *Reformation* had appeared January 12, 1642. Now fifty years old, Comenius had astonished all Europe with the success of his Latin textbook, *Januarum Linguarum Reserata* (1631), which had been translated into twelve languages. The sixth edition in English appeared in 1641 and again in 1643. The *Janua* consisted of one thousand Latin sentences, divided into one hundred categories of ten sentences each, on such topics as fruits, herbs, stones, birds, water creatures; opposite each Latin sentence appeared its English equivalent. Like his master Bacon, Comenius emphasized sensory language: "Things are the same to all." Still more vital to Comenius was the artifice of gradation: "Every man is able to get to the top of an high Tower . . . if there be steps for him." In this principle lay Comenius' hope for the weakest mind, the most sluggish child.

## 62. Milton on Educational Reform

HARDLY had Milton completed his second edition of *Doctrine and Discipline of Divorce* (published February 2, 1644) than he responded to Hartlib's fervent pleas to set forth his ideas of educational reform. The opening lines of *Of Education. To Master Samuel Hartlib* (June 5, 1644) show that Milton was by no means ready to write such a tract, though education "be one of the greatest and noblest designes, that can be thought on, and for the want whereof this nation perishes." Nor

will he review, he tells Hartlib, what he has learned from old authors about education; and to search through later books, the "modern *Janua's* and *Didactics* more then ever I shall read . . . my inclination leads me not." It is evident that Hartlib has pressed Milton very hard to give Comenian ideas a passage, however brief, into his capacious mind. To Comenius nothing was fixed in human nature except teachability; man was limited not so much by genetic deficiency as by society's failure to provide small steps by which a child could rise to a great height. No such democratic assumptions appealed to Milton in 1644; his emphasis was on the select few from cultivated families. In 1660, however, when the Commonwealth was toppling, Milton spoke out for a revolutionary democratic plan: English citizens should have "schools and academies at thir own choice, wherin thir children may be bred up in thir own sight to all learning and noble education not in grammar only, but in all liberal arts and exercises." Only in a commonwealth, asserted Milton, could such an educational plan become a reality; monarchs would never permit it.

(1)

## Of Education.   To Master *Samuel Hartlib.*

Master Hartlib,

 Am long since perswaded, that to say, or doe ought worth memory, and imitation, no purpose or respect should sooner move us, then simply the love of God, and of mankinde. Neverthelesse to write now the reforming of Education, though it be one of the greatest and noblest designes, that can be thought on, and for the want whereof this nation perishes, I had not yet at this time been induc't, but by your earnest entreaties, and serious conjurements; as having my minde for the present halfe diverted in the persuance of some other assertions, the knowledge and the use of which, cannot but be a great furtherance both to the enlargement of truth, and honest living, with much more peace. Nor should the lawes of any private friendship have prevail'd with me to divide thus, or transpose my former thoughts, but that I see those aims, those actions which have won you with me the esteem of a person sent hither by some good providence from a farre country to be the occasion and the incitement of great good to this Iland. And, as I hear, you have obtain'd the same repute with men of most approved wisdom, and some of highest authority among us. Not to mention the learned correspondence which you hold in forreigne parts, and the extraordinary pains and diligence which you have us'd in this matter both heer, and beyond the Seas; either by the definite will of God so ruling, or the peculiar sway of nature, which also is Gods working. Neither can I thinke that so reputed, and so valu'd as you are, you would

63A

63B

## 63. Cromwell at Marston Moor

ON July 2, 1644, in a three-hour battle seven miles west of York, the Parliamentary forces met and routed the royalist army under the command of Prince Rupert. Over four thousand men lost their lives, the royalists suffering more heavily than their enemies. Three days after the battle, Cromwell, now lieutenant general and second in command to Essex, wrote to his brother-in-law, "The left wing, which I commanded, being our own horse, saving a few Scots in our rear, beat all the Prince's horse. God gave them as stubble to our swords. We charged their regiments of foot with our horse, and routed all we charged." Within a few days the news reached London. The names of Cromwell and the "men of a spirit" he commanded were already becoming a legend.

## 64. Rising Secular Tones: The *Areopagitica*

ON November 24, 1644, appeared Milton's most profoundly revolutionary pamphlet, extending the principle of religious toleration to the whole spectrum of secular dilemmas: "Give me the liberty to know, to utter, and to argue freely according to conscience, above all liberties." A book, however absurd or monstrous in ideas, deserves the gift of life; let no jury condemn it ere it be born into the world. "As good almost kill a Man as kill a good Book," which is "the pretious life-blood of a master spirit, imbalm'd and treasur'd up on purpose to a life beyond life." Milton sent forth his prose masterpiece, as he had *Doctrine and Discipline*, in defiance of the new printing ordinance passed by Parliament on June 14, 1643. But *Areopagitica* was far more heretical than the divorce tracts. Not the tumbling of the bishops, or religious reformation alone, should content us: "If . . . the rule of life both economicall and politicall be not lookt into and reform'd . . . we are stark blind." In calling for secular reformation, Milton insisted that the need for open debating was more urgent than ever: when all presses are open, and all men free to speak, truth will rise triumphant, itself the most potent censor in the world.

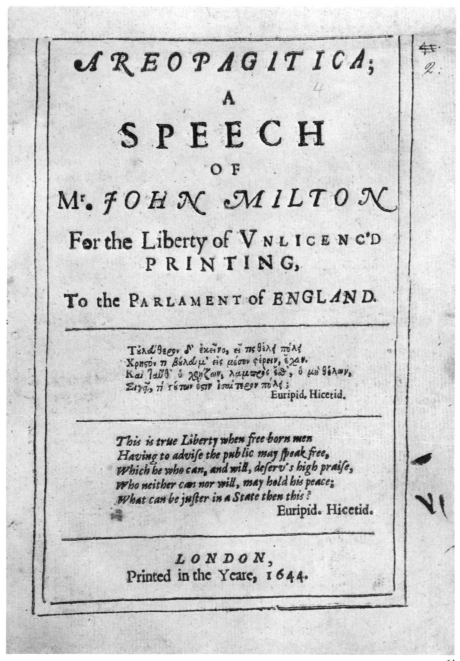

65

## 65. Execution of Archbishop Laud

AFTER languishing three years in prison, Archbishop Laud was finally brought to trial March 12, 1644. The longer the war continued, the greater the hatred for him among the Puritan ministers, whether Presbyterian or Independent. Sermons before the Parliament cried out for the old man's blood in the name of God's justice. After a trial of over nine months Laud was finally convicted and sentenced to execution, barely escaping the ignominy of hanging. On January 10, 1645, seventy-two years old, he ascended the scaffold on Tower Hill, gave his sermon, said goodbye to his friends, and bravely laid his head upon the block.

## 66. The Battle of Naseby

THE first baptism of fire for the New Model Army, now structured according to the wishes of Cromwell and his colleagues in the Commons, took place on the early morning of June 14, 1645, in the battle of Naseby. The royalist army, commanded by King Charles and Prince Rupert, was utterly routed by Parliament's forces, now under the command of Sir Thomas Fairfax. Five thousand royalist soldiers were taken prisoner, including many of the king's key officers. All of Charles's artillery fell into Parliament's hands; but equally important was the capture of the king's cabinet of official papers and private correspondence. Published at once by Parliament as *The King's Cabinet Opened*, the papers revealed Charles's secret negotiations with the Irish and the influence of the queen in the king's decisions. As at Marston Moor, Cromwell had commanded the horse on the right wing; the colonels he had trained were now all but invincible. The victorious left wing had been led by Henry Ireton (soon to become a portent of Puritan triumphs), promoted at Cromwell's suggestion to Commissary General of Horse only the night before the battle.

The train guarded with firelocks

NASBYE

Printed for John Patridge

66A

66B

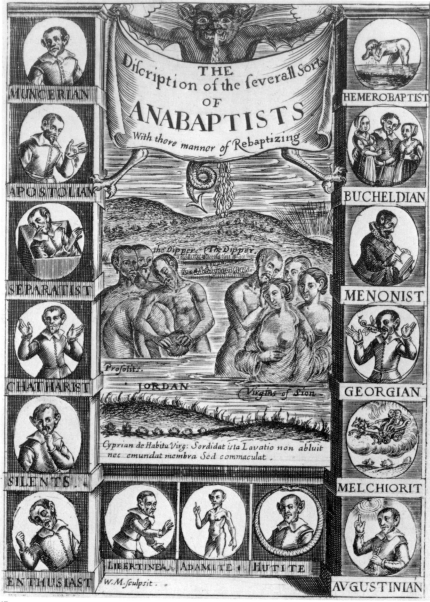

67

## 67. Sectarians in the New Model

MANY of Cromwell's best soldiers were men of strange opinions in religion, which soon led to expression of secular heresies as well. Each victory instilled greater confidence in a soldier's interpretation of the Bible, especially if he were a man of humble birth. "When I came to the army, among Cromwell's soldiers," wrote Richard Baxter, "I found a new face of things which I never dreamt of: I heard the plotting heads very hot upon that which intimated their intention to subvert both Church and State. Independency and Anabaptistry were most prevalent; Antinomian-

ism and Arminianism were equally distributed. . . . Abundance of the common troopers, and many of the officers, I found to be honest, sober, orthodox men . . . but a few proud, self-conceited, hot-headed sectaries had got into the highest places, and were Cromwell's chief favourites, and by their heat and activity bore down the rest . . . and were the soul of the Army. . . . They said, What were the Lords of England but William the Conquerer's colonels?" Thus, around the campfires revolutionary dialogue waxed apace; and the essence of *Areopagitica*, the right "to know, to utter, to argue freely," was realized more fully than in any other army of English history.

## 68. The Damnable Tenets of Tradesmen

On April 26, 1647, appeared a broadside attributing dangerous heresies to humble tradesmen, suggesting indeed that the more menial the worker the more susceptible he was to the propaganda of the political and theological left. Did not some benighted tradesmen even claim that "Christs blood did not purchase Heaven for any man"? Moreover, any heaven we may find, asserted the tradesmen, is here on earth. To them there was no sin in adultery or drunkenness or breaking the Sabbath. Some sectaries claimed that if any man worshipped the sun or the moon, no one should censure him or say him nay. Such were the damnable beliefs of shoemakers, soap boilers, button makers, porters, boxmakers, spreading about London in this troubled age.

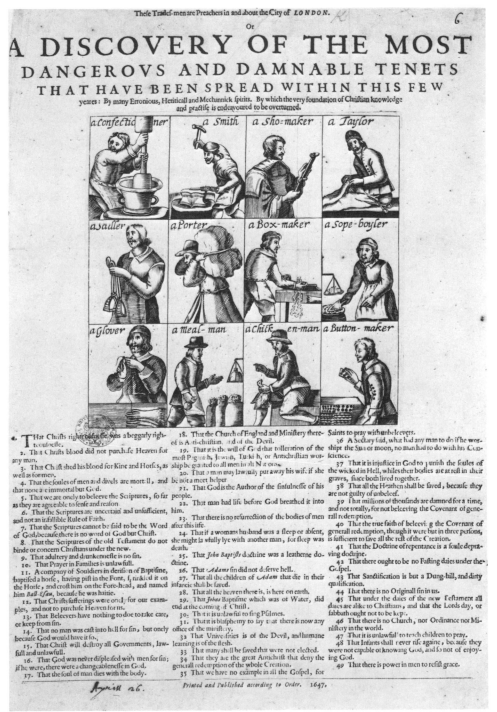

69

## 69. Cromwell Writes to Lenthall

CROMWELL was well aware that the Presbyterian majority in the Commons looked with dismay at the rise of Independency and the spread of sectarian agitation in the New Model Army. Even before leaving Naseby field, June 14, 1645, Cromwell wrote to Speaker Lenthall: "Honest men served you faithfully in this action. Sir, they are trusty; I beseech you, in the name of God, not to discourage them. . . . He that ventures his life for the liberty of his country, I wish he may trust God for the liberty of his conscience, and you for the liberty he fights for." In these words Cromwell spoke for an extreme tolerationist principle neither Parliament nor citizens at large were prepared to accept; but for the moment victories on the battlefield were a reality of irresistible persuasion.

## 70. The Flight of the King

AFTER long months of irresolution following the Naseby catastrophe, King Charles finally decided to put himself under the protection of the Scottish army at Newark. But on April 27, 1646, disguised as a servant, still uncertain about his plans, accompanied only by John Ashburnham and Dr. Hudson, a clergyman, the king rode out of Oxford toward London by way of Henley, Brentford, and Harrow-on-the-Hill. His purpose wavering, Charles now turned north toward St. Albans, then eastward into Norfolk, where he stopped at Downham four or five days, from April 30 to May 4. All England now knew about the king's flight; a proclamation was issued denouncing anyone who harbored him as a traitor. On May 5 Charles returned to his original plan and sought haven with the Scots' army at Newark. Fearing an attack from the New Model Army that might endanger the king, the Scots on May 13 withdrew northward to Newcastle.

The Pourtraicture of his Excellency Sr: Thomas Farfax Generall of all the English forces for the Service of ye: two houses of Parliament.

Guill. Faithorne Sculp:

71

## 71. The King's Forts and Cities Surrender

THE king's forces were now scattered and help-less; the war was virtually at an end. On June 10, 1646, Charles sent out orders from Newcastle to his commanders to surrender their cities and cas-tles. Oxford was surrendered to Fairfax on June 24, followed by the surrender of Worcester on July 22, Wallingford Castle on July 27, Pen-dennis Castle of Cornwall on August 17, Raglan Castle, August 19.

## 72. *Poems of Mr. John Milton* ... *1645*

On January 2, 1646, the publisher Humphrey Moseley issued the first edition of Milton's poetry, divided into two parts separately paged, *English Poems* (120 pp.) and Latin poems, *Joannis Miltoni Londoniensis Poemata* (87 pp.). The Nativity Ode opens the *English Poems*, which include "On Shakespear. 1630," "Song on May Morning," "L'Allegro," and "Il Penseroso," followed by ten English and Italian sonnets. Then appear "Arcades," "Lycidas," and *Comus* (the last with a separate title page). The *Poemata* are themselves divided into two parts, the *Elegies*, numbered I to VII, followed by five epigrams on the Gunpowder Plot and three bits of verse on Leonora Baroni. A second part, called *Sylvarum Liber*, contains "In Quintum Novembris," "Ad Patrem," and four other Cambridge poems, followed by verses written in Italy, "Ad Salsillum" and "Mansus." At the end of *Sylvarum Liber* appears "Epitaphium Damonis," Milton's moving tribute to Diodati, written upon his return to England.

Joannis Miltoni

LONDINENSIS

POEMATA.

Quorum pleraque intra
Annum ætatis Vigesimum
Conscripsit.

Nunc primum Edita.

LONDINI,
Typis *R. R.* Prostant ad Insignia Principis,
in Cœmeterio D. *Pauli,* apud *Humphredum
Moseley.* 1 6 4 5.

---

POEMS

OF

Mr. *John Milton,*

BOTH

ENGLISH and LATIN,
Compos'd at several times.

Printed by *his true Copies.*

The Songs were set in Musick by
Mr. HENRY LAWES Gentleman of
the KINGS Chappel, and one
of His MAIESTIES
Private Musick.

—— *Baccare frontem*
*Cingite, ne vati noceat mala lingua futuro,*
Virgil, Eclog. 7.

Printed and publish'd according to
ORDER.

LONDON,
Printed by *Ruth Raworth* for *Humphrey Moseley,*
and are to be sold at the signe of the Princes
Arms in *Pauls* Church-yard. 1645.

73

## 73. Joyce's Arrest of the King

BY AGREEMENT with the Scots, Parliament's commissioners had taken possession of the king at Newcastle on January 30, 1647, and removed him to Holmby House in Northamptonshire. But on February 19 the Commons in a close vote (158-148) had decided to disband the New Model infantry, allowing only a small force of troopers to maintain garrisons throughout the country. At this news Cromwell's army seethed with agitation. Two agitators were selected from each regiment of horse to represent the wishes of the common soldiers. Manifestoes, printed almost daily by Leveller leaders and distributed among the soldiers, called for far-reaching reforms. In the struggle between the will of the Presbyterian Parliament and the army dominated by Independents and unpredictable sects, men saw that the possession of the king would be crucial in the oncoming struggle. On June 3, acting without orders, Cornet George Joyce, of Fairfax's lifeguard, led a body of troopers to Holmby House, gained access to the king against the protests of the commissioners, and persuaded him to leave Holmby with his troopers next afternoon.

## 74. *An Agreement of the People*

On October 29, 1647, the General Council of the Army (consisting of the chief officers and the Agitators elected by each regiment) met to discuss a proposed new constitution for England, *An Agreement of the People*. Fortunately the remarkable debate that followed was preserved in shorthand; twenty-five decades later it was published verbatim by Sir Charles Firth in *Clarke Papers*. The *Agreement* was intended to be distributed and signed by all Englishmen over twenty-one (whether propertied or penniless) as the source of political power. Cromwell and Ireton led the debate against this revolutionary proposal; Colonel Rainsborough spoke brilliantly for it. Not property but reason, he asserted, qualified a man to vote, and reason was the endowment of the humblest man in England.

AN
AGREEMENT
OF THE
PEOPLE
FOR
A firme and present Peace, upon
grounds of common-right and free-
dome;

As it was proposed by the Agents of the five
Regiments of Horse; and since by the generall approba-
tion of the Army, offered to the joynt concurrence of all the free Commons of
England.

The Names of the Regiments which have already appeared for the
Case, of *The Case of the Army truly stated*, and for this
present Agreement, VIZ.

1. Gen. Regiment.
2. Life-Guard.
3. Lieut. Gen. Regiment.
4. Com. Gen. Regiment,
5. Col. Whaleyes Reg.
6. Col. Rickes Reg.
7. Col. Fleetwoods Reg.
8. Col. Harrisons Reg.
9. Col. Twisldens Reg.

Of Horse

1. Gen. Regiment.
2. Col. Sir Hardresse
Wallers Reg.
3. Col. Lamberts Reg.
4. Col. Rainsboroughs Regiment.
5. Col. Overtons Reg.
6. Col. Lilburns Reg.
7. Col. Backsters Reg.

Of Foot.

Printed Anno Dom. 1647.

## 75. Cromwell Suppresses a Mutiny

ABOUT two-thirds of Cromwell's army were now avowed supporters of the Leveller constitutional solution as set forth in the *Agreement of the People*. At the rendezvous held at Corkbush Field, near Ware, on November 15, 1647, the soldiers of two regiments, those commanded by Harrison and Robert Lilburne, appeared on the field with copies of the *Agreement* stuck in their hats. When Fairfax and his fellow officers spoke to the two regiments, finally ordering them to remove the mutinous manifesto, Harrison's regiment good-humoredly complied; but Lilburne's regiment sullenly refused. After shouts of admonition, Cromwell dashed among the soldiers with drawn sword. Then, selecting three of the leaders, he had them tried by summary court-martial on the field; the three men drew lots to select the comrade to be executed. As the soldier Arnold sank to the ground after the fatal shots, the men had learned their lesson. The resolute discipline of war had dissolved their agitation for a democratic compact.

76B

76C

76A

## 76. Charles Rejects the Four Bills

THE Four Bills passed by Parliament on December 14, 1647, asserted its power over the militia for twenty years, required that the king confirm its actions in the Civil War, withdrew the peerages he had conferred since hostilities began, and left the crucial decisions of adjournment in the hands of the two Houses. In essence the Four Bills embodied in their bowels a constitutional revolution; Charles could not consent. The Scottish Commissioners not only sided with Charles's adamant refusal; on December 26 they made a secret treaty with him whereby he agreed to confirm the Covenant, abolish Episcopacy, establish Presbyterian church government throughout England, suppress the Independents and other sects, all these actions on condition that the Scottish army invade England and place him again on the throne of the two nations.

# The Second Civil War: Milton and King Charles

### 77. Royalist Sentiment Still Pervasive

DESPITE Charles's rejection of the Four Bills, he still commanded the loyalty of the citizens at large; it was impossible for the average subject to conceive of a settlement that would not include a return of Charles to the throne. In the House of Commons, as in the country at large, Presbyterian sentiment was dominantly royalist. In the months of May through August, 1648, it was not hard for Charles and his Scottish allies to organize a series of uprisings. Many royalist exiles returned to England from abroad. In greater or less degree, men wanted to limit the king's power; but they visualized no stability until he was returned to the throne. Only Cromwell and his sectarian army stood in the way of an accommodation with the monarch. Yet many men, in Parliament and out, were proud of Cromwell, too, and his victories over the Cavaliers. Was not the Lord on Cromwell's side? His proud claim, "God made them as stubble to our swords," was no idle boast to the pious Presbyterians.

THE HUMBLE
PETITION
OF THE
Lord Major, Aldermen, and Commons
of the City of LONDON,
IN
Common-Councell
ASSEMBLED,

Presented to the Right Honourable
THE
LORDS and COMMONS
in Parliament Assembled:

WITH
The Answer of the Lords to the said
PETITION.

Printed by RICHARD COTES, Printer to the
Honorable City of London, August 8. 1648.

Major General Ireton
1650

78A

## 78. A Momentous Prayer Meeting

In March or April, 1648, when the Second Civil War seemed imminent, Cromwell called a prayer meeting of his chief officers. The army, all agreed, was in "a low, weak, divided, perplexed condition." Looking back, said Cromwell, on the second day of the prayer meeting, was there one moment of time they could point to unanimously when the Lord had withdrawn his face and favor from them? On the third day the choice of such a moment did emerge: the time when they decided to have conferences with the king. The king's forces were now again rising up against them. The officers decided, wrote one of their number long afterward, "that it was our duty, if ever the Lord brought us back again in peace, to call Charles Stuart, that man of blood, to an account for that blood he had shed, and mischief he had done to his utmost, against the Lord's Cause and People in these poor Nations." Thus were the officers first resolved to call their king to judgment; and in the Commons Thomas Scott declared that no peace was possible with "so perfidious and implacable a prince" as Charles I.

A FAITHFUL
# MEMORIAL
OF THAT
## REMARKABLE MEETING
OF
Many Officers of the Army in *England*,
at *Windsor* Castle, in the Year 1648.

AS ALSO,
# A DISCOVERY
OF THE
Great goodnefs of God, in his gracious meeting of them, hearing and anfwering their fuit or fupplications, while they were yet fpeaking to him.

ALL
Which is humbly prefented, as a precious Patern and Prefident unto the Officers and Souldiers of the faid Army (or elfewhere) who are or fhall be found in the like path, of following the Lord in this evil day; fearching and trying their waies, in order to a through Return and Reformation.

By *William Allen*, late Adjutant-General of the Army in *Ireland*.

Prov. 1. 23. *Turn you at my reproof: behold, I will pour out my spirit unto you, I will make known my words unto you.*

LONDON,
Printed for *Livewel Chapman*, at the Crown in *Popes-head* Alley. 1659. *April 27*

78B

## 79. England for the King

It has been said that Cromwell fought the Second Civil War "with a rope around his neck." Parliament was more concerned with putting down sectaries than resisting the army of Scots. Only on July 14, 1648, when the Commons realized that Hamilton's Scots were invading English soil, did it act to declare the invaders enemies of the state or those Englishmen traitors who assisted them. Even so, the Lords refused to concur! Royalist sentiment pervaded the land, supported by Presbyterian agitation, especially in London. One royalist agitator spoke of the Cromwellian faction as "The Mad Dog Rebellion" that had "resisted God, offended the King, and ruined the Kingdome."

**(1)**

## The Mad Dog REBELLION, worm'd and muzzl'd.

*With some Reasons why a Personall Treaty with his Majesty is delayed, why held in doubt or suspence, and why never like to be, if some can withstand it.*

IT is an exceeding joy, and cause of continuall thankfullnesse to God, of and for all loyall Subjects, for having the happinesse to have so much grace given them from above, as not to be Rebells; but (in bad time be it spoken) *England* is now, and hath beene a long time plagued with them as the *Egyptians* were with incumerable Frogs, Lice, and Caterpillers, &c. As they are *Englishmen* they are to be loved, and pittied, but as they are Rebells they are to be abhor'd; they are to be grieved for (as Brethren) but they are to be opposed as the worst of Enemies: as we ought to require them to a loyall peace; so also we should desire them to be all hang'd if they continue obstinate, bloody Rebells.

Let us examine and conferre a little with our selves, could any, or all the forraigne enemies we have, ever have done this once famous and Renowned Kingdome so much mischiefe as we have done and suffered more then 7 yeares? Thele barbarous Villaines do know that they were never called of God, and they know also they were never sent by the King; they further know that by their Rebellion they have resisted God, offended the King, and ruined the Kingdome; and all this they have done under the pretence of Reformation, and under the colour or pretence of Gods cause, and the Kings honour, and their Countreys good, Kim Kam, against all Law and order of God and man: are they Kings to rule and governe? Let us know how, and by whose permission: Are they the Kings Officers, or Ministers?

*July. 13. 1648*  A

79

80

## 80. The Battle of Preston

ON EVERY hand, however, the disciplined forces of Cromwell, Fairfax, and Lambert overwhelmed the enemy. On August 17, 1648, after joining forces with Lambert's army in Yorkshire, Cromwell intercepted the southward march of Hamilton's army of Scots and English, some 24,000 men, with 9,000 tested veterans of the New Model. In the three-day battle of Preston that followed, the Scots and their English allies were utterly destroyed by the Puritan army. Three thousand of the enemy were taken prisoner. Other thousands fled northward in despair along the country roads, pleading for bread along the way. Hamilton, with a small group of attending officers and soldiers, surrendered in Staffordshire on August 25.

## 81. Pride's Purge

HAVING now defeated the king's forces a second time, the army was resolved to bring him to judgment, even against the will of the Presbyterian majority of the Commons. To this end the army chose a desperate expedient: a purging of the Commons of members hostile to their aims. On the morning of December 6, 1648, under orders of Fairfax and the General Council of Officers, Colonel Thomas Pride blocked all the entrances to the House of Commons with two or three regiments of soldiers. Holding a list of the names in his hand, Pride caused forty-seven members of the Commons to be arrested and ninety-six others to be turned away. It was an ominous portent for the future of constitutional government. Young Henry Vane was as indignant as the most rigid Presbyterian. Henceforward called the Rump Parliament, the Commons, meeting daily, continued to follow the ancient forms. As events were to show, Pride's Purge had Milton's complete approval; like Cromwell he cared not a rush for broken links in England's constitutional tradition.

## 82. A Constitutional Revolution

EVENTS now moved forward with startling suddenness. On January 4 the Commons resolved that their members, chosen by the people, "have the supreme power in this nation," without consent of monarch or House of Lords. On January 6 a revised ordinance for the High Court of Justice was passed, naming 135 "judicial commissioners" charged with the responsibility of trying the king. The names of Fairfax, Cromwell, and Ireton stood at the head of the list. On January 9 a new Great Seal was ordered engraved, with the legend "The Great Seal of England: 1648" on one side; and on the other, "In the First Year of Freedom by God's blessing restored: 1648."

83A

83B

83C

A Description of the High Court of Justice : 1648

## 83. The Trial of Charles I

ON Saturday, January 20, 1649, the trial of Charles was opened in Cotton House, adjoining Westminster Hall. The president of the court was John Bradshaw; sixty-seven judges were present, including Cromwell, Ireton, Marten, and Ludlow. The charge against the king was that he had "traitorously and maliciously levied war against the present Parliament and the People therein represented." Repeatedly interrupted by Bradshaw, Charles denied that the court had any jurisdiction over him; he refused to plead either guilty or not guilty. According to English cus- tom, a man should be tried by a jury of his peers. But was any man there his peer? asked the king. *"I speak not for my own Right alone,"* he de- clared, *". . . but also for the true Liberty of all My Subjects."* The trial lasted seven days, at the end of which President Bradshaw pronounced the sentence: *"This Court doth adjudge that he the said Charles Stuart, as a Tyrant, Traitor, Mur- derer, and a Public Enemy, shall be put to death by the severing of his head from his body."* In vain did Charles try to speak both before and after the sentence. Not for a moment did he show anger or confusion, even when the guards roughly surrounded him and forced him to with- draw from the Hall.

O horrible Murder

But lo a Charg is drawne a day is set
The silent lamb is brought, the wolves are met;
And where's the Slaughter-house. Whitehall must be,
Lately his Palace, now his Calvarie
And now ye Senators is this the thing
So oft declar'd is this your glorious King?
Religion vails her self, and mourns that she
Is forc'd to own such Horrid Villanie.

84A

84B

## 84. Execution of the King

ABOUT noon on January 30, 1649, Colonel Andrew Hacker (to whom the death warrant of Charles had been delivered) came with a guard of soldiers to Whitehall, where Charles had passed the night, attended by Bishop Juxon and Sir Thomas Herbert. The king was then led to the New Banqueting Hall, where a large crowd had gathered; a murmur of sympathy swept over the people. Through a window removed from the wall Charles passed outside to the scaffold erected on the street, surrounded now by a dense crowd of spectators and companies of soldiers. On the scaf-fold hung with black, men could see in the center the block, the axe, and several executioners in black masks. Stiff and unflinching, Charles spoke briefly to the crowd, asserting again the legal basis of his kingly rights and his undying loyalty to the Church of England. Then, taking the white cap from Juxon, Charles placed it on his head; with the help of the bishop and the executioner, the king's long hair was at last confined within the cap's rim. Finally, taking off his cloak and handing it to Juxon, uttering the one word, "Remember," Charles knelt down and laid his head upon the block. After a brief moment the king stretched out his arms, whereupon the executioner struck off his head in one blow.

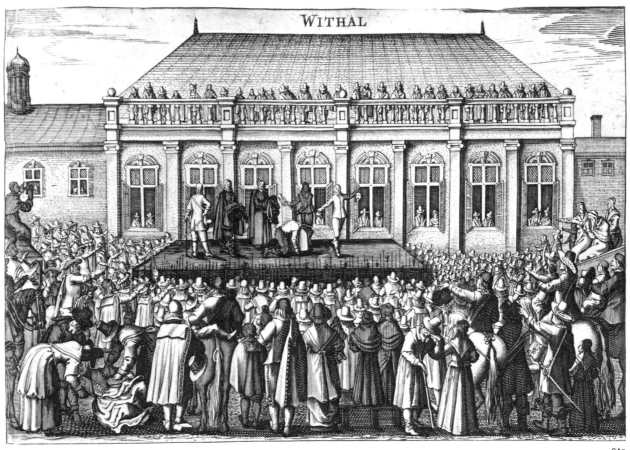

WITHAL

84C

BANCKET HAVS

84D

## 85. Milton Writes *The Tenure*

MILTON's sympathies were heart and soul with the men who had brought Charles to trial and sentenced him to death on the scaffold. The poet cared no more than Cromwell or Peters for constitutional precedent. Even while the trial was in progress (it is thought) Milton was at work on his justification of the Rump's action, asserting that "it is Lawfull, and hath been . . . through all Ages, for any, who have the Power, to call to account a Tyrant, or wicked KING, and after due conviction, to depose, and put him to death." Milton's sharpest animus is directed at the Presbyterian ministers and lay leaders who have fought against Charles, "curs'd him all over in thir Pulpits and thir Pamphlets," but now fall back defensively on "that old entanglement of Iniquity, thir gibrish Lawes." Charles, after all the shedding of innocent blood, still obdurate and impenitent, is now again to the Presbyterians "the Lords anointed, not to be touch'd, though by themselves imprison'd." Throughout the *Tenure* runs the thread of reasoning that man is born free, endowed with the right to join with his fellows in compact to govern themselves and "bind each other from mutual injury." But for a citizen to put himself in one man's power above the law is no better than submitting oneself to the reign of a savage beast. In such vein spoke *The Tenure of Kings and Magistrates*, which appeared in London February 13, 1649, about thirteen days after the execution of Charles I.

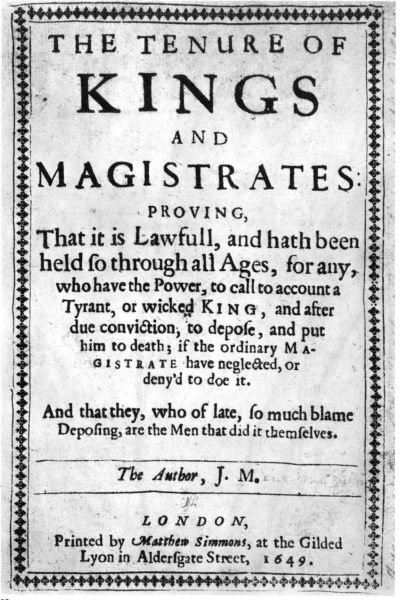

## 86. Milton as Latin Secretary

On March 13, 1649, Milton was invited by the new Council of State to become "Secretary for the Foreign Tongues." Milton was now forty-one, at the height of his powers, eager to concentrate on his beloved literary endeavors. Yet he could not refuse a place among the leaders of the new republic. The Council met daily in Whitehall, usually at seven A.M. Milton's work as Latin Secretary soon broadened to other duties. Within a few weeks he was asked to reply to *Eikon Basilike*, an incredibly popular defense of the king, written as autobiography, which had appeared only ten days after the execution. Milton's reply, *Eikonoklastes*, passionate and scholarly, which appeared October 6, 1649, possessed no such magic as that of the *Basilike*, purportedly written by Charles himself (actually by Dr. John Gauden) in the shadow of the scaffold and the axe of the executioner.

ΕΙΚΟΝΟΚΛΑΣΤΗΣ
IN
# Anſwer
To a Book Intitl'd
ΕΙΚΩΝ ΒΑΣΙΛΙΚΗ,
THE
PORTRATURE of his Sacred MAJESTY
in his *Solitudes* and *Sufferings*.

The Author   I. M. *ilton*.

PROV. 28. 15, 16, 17.

15. *As a roaring Lyon, and a ranging Beare, ſo is a wicked Ruler over the poor people.*
16. *The Prince that wanteth underſtanding, is alſo a great oppreſſor; but he that hateth covetouſneſſe ſhall prolong his dayes.*
17. *A man that doth violence to the blood of any perſon, ſhall fly to the pit, let no man ſtay him.*

*Saluſt. Conjurat. Catilin.*

Regium imperium, quod initio, conſervandæ libertatis, atque augendæ reipub. cauſâ fuerat, in ſuperbiam, dominationemque ſe convertit.
Regibus boni, quam mali, ſuſpectiores ſunt; ſemperque his aliena virtus formidoloſa eſt.
Quidlibet impunè facere, hoc ſcilicet regium eſt.

*Publiſhed by Authority.*

*London*, Printed by *Matthew Simmons*, next dore to the gilded Lyon in Alderſgate ſtreet. 1649.

86B

86A

## JOANNIS MILTONI
### Angli
#### PRO POPULO ANGLICANO
## DEFENSIO

Contra *Claudii Anonymi*, aliàs *Salmasii*,
Defensionem REGIAM.

*LONDINI*,
Typis *Du-Gardianis*. Anno Domini 1651.

87

## 87. Milton's Reply to the Great Salmasius

ON January 8, 1650, Milton was asked by the Council of State to answer the *Defensio Regia* of the great French scholar Salmasius, which had appeared before November, 1649. By the early months of 1650, though Milton had already lost the sight of his left eye, he pushed forward steadily on the composition of his *Defence of the English People*, pitting the vast range of his learning against that of his antagonist, upholding the new republic, which he compared to the great free commonwealths of Greece and Rome. By the time *A Defence* appeared, February 24, 1651, the sight of Milton's right eye was woefully diminished. But profound as Milton's dedication was to the new republic, his great epic still voiceless and unstructured, he had no regrets and no doubts of ultimate victory over all obstacles to his creative ends.

## 88. The Battle of Dunbar

IN THE spring of 1650 the Scots were gathering their forces for a new invasion of England. Supreme commander after the resignation of Fairfax in June, 1650, Cromwell marched north to meet the army of Scots commanded by the resourceful David Leslie. Near Dunbar, on September 2, 1650, when Cromwell saw the enemy regrouping on ground lower than his own, he resolved instantly to attack. Next morning at sunrise the 12,000 horse and foot of the English army fell upon the enemy, a force of 22,000. Cromwell's seasoned veterans soon forced a retreat that dissolved almost at once into a rout. Cromwell shouted, "Let God arise, let His enemies be scattered!" Three thousand Scots perished; 10,000 were taken captive. According to Cromwell, the English lost scarce twenty men.

88A

88B

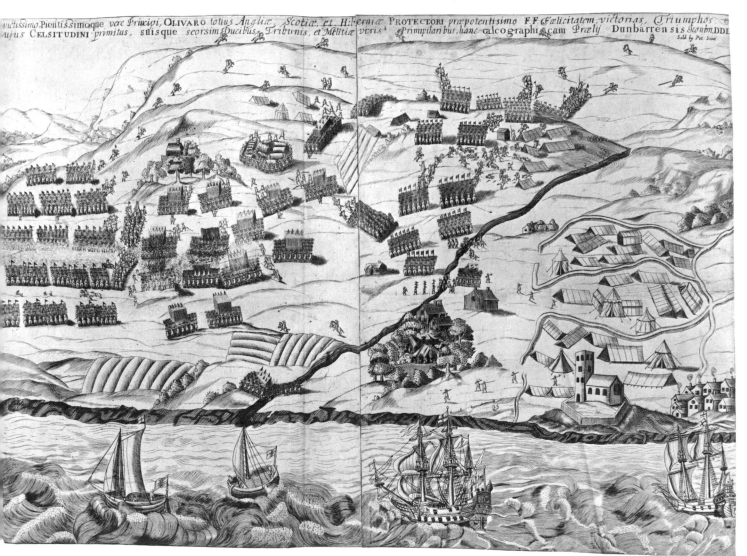

88C

## 89. The Battle of Worcester

WITHIN a year after Dunbar the Scots, led now by Charles II, were again ready to invade England. In this emergency Cromwell's strategy was to withdraw before the advance of the Scots, meanwhile harassing their march, augmenting his forces with the county militias, and awaiting the moment to strike again with his tested veterans, this time on English soil. On September 3, 1651, the first anniversary of Dunbar, Cromwell's men crossed the rivers Teme and Severn and breached the defenses of Worcester. The Scots, led by Charles, fought bravely and well, yielding gradually street by street, tower after tower, finally Fort Royal itself. Once outside the city, the enemy found fresh militia stationed at every bridge, every road. Of the famous Scot leaders, including Hamilton, Leslie, Middleton, and Massie, none escaped except, miraculously, Charles himself, who had fought bravely and well at the head of his troops. Cromwell reported six or seven thousand prisoners. "Indeed it was a stiff business," he wrote; "yet I do not think we lost two-hundred men." When defeat of the enemy seemed inevitable, Cromwell rode up and down the lines, exhorting the Scots to surrender. The victory was, he wrote, "for aught I know, a crowning mercy." Never again in Cromwell's time would Scotland challenge the might of English arms.

*Charles y 2d was proclaymed King of great Britain France & Ireland at Worcester: 23d Augᵘ: 1651 .*

## 90. Milton and *Mercurius Politicus*

BY January, 1651, Milton was acting as censor of *Mercurius Politicus*, the official weekly newspaper of the Commonwealth, edited by Marchamont Needham, whom Milton had rescued from prison and persuaded to write for the new republic. Beginning in January, 1651, a number of leading articles show traces of Milton's participation in the writing of *Politicus*. Nowhere is this more evident than in the issue of September 4-11, 1651, just after the great victory at Worcester. Does this victory not show afresh, asks the writer, that God is on the side of the new republic? Remember Naseby, continues the commentator, was it not "a loud *Declaration* from Heaven" of the Lord's support? Similarly, God was with the army that overthrew Hamilton's proud soldiery, "re-setled the whole Nation, and brought the *King* to the Bar and Block of Justice." And what of Dunbar? Was this great triumph not a sign of the Lord's continued favor? There "a wearied and sick handfull of men, coop't in a nook of Land within the Arms of the Sea" put to rout the numerous Scots. In such victories, asserted the writer, "several links in this great Chain of Mercies," God has traced with "his own Finger" his intentions for England's future.

# Mercurius Politicus.

## Comprising the summe of all Intelligence, with the Affairs and Designs now on foot in the three Nations of England, Ireland, and Scotland.

### In defence of the Common-wealth, and for Information of the People.

——— Ità vertere Seria. {Hor. de Ar Poet

P.P. London.
K

From *Thursday* Septemb. 4. to *Thursday* Septemb. 11. 1651.

F after so many eminent discoveries of the will and purpose of God, touching the establishment of this *Commonwealth* any man shall yet be so much a *Sot*, as to continue a *Malignant*, let him remember how God useth to dispose of his incorrigible and implacable Enemies. But I perceive, one main impediment that keeps men from quitting their old corrupt principles, is, the Fear of being counted a *Turn-Coat*: yet know, that if God once declare as it were from Heaven against thy wayes, thy Principles, or thy Party, then it is no dishonor, but Ingenuity, and thy duty to Turn: For, he hath said in this case; *If a man doe not turn, he will whet his Sword, he hath bent his Bow, and made it ready: he hath prepared for him the instruments of death and destruction.*

It was a loud *Declaration* from Heaven at *Naseby*, when

Qqqqqq                                    by

90A

by a despised Company it pleased God to decide the controversie; and also in the year 1647. when God owned this *Cause*, against a powerfull faction both in *Parliament* and *City*. But in the year 1648. he spake louder, in the midst of all those Alarms and *Insurrections*, when by a small handfull he overthrew *Hamilton's* numerous proud Army in *Lancashire*, re-setled the whole Nation, and brought the *King* to the Bar and Block of Justice. Remember how eminently he hath appeared since, both in *Ireland* and *Scotland*, by many miraculous successes; but especially at *Dunbarr*, where by a wearied and sick handfull of men, coop't in a nook of Land within the Arms of the Sea, & encompass't with extreme disadvantages, hee was pleased so visibly to make bare his own Arm, and give a totall Foile to that numerous *Scotish* Army in their own Country; where being well accomplisht, and provided, both with Numbers and Necessaries, they reckoned Themselvs sure of spoil and Victory. In all these Particulars, and many other since, God did sufficiently signify his own will and pleasure, but his loudest *Declaration* of all was mightily set forth in the late sudden Revolutions and Actions, before, and at *Worcester*; whereby he unquestionably

90B

## 91. Milton's Growing Renown

ON July 26, 1651, Mr. Christopher Arnold, a German traveller of distinction, wrote to Dr. George Richter, Vice-Chancellor of the University of Altorf, about remarkable learned men he had met in England, among them John Selden, James Ussher, William Petty, and John Milton. Arnold wrote that Milton "enters readily into talk," also that "his style is pure and his writing most terse." On November 19, 1651, Milton signed Arnold's *Album Amicorum* after having dictated to a friend or amanuensis the inscription reproduced below. The opening sentence in Greek (an approximate rendition of 2 Corinthians 12:9) reads thus: "My strength is made perfect in weakness." The firm signature is undeniably Milton's own, showing that his eyesight had not completely faded.

## 92. Milton in Total Darkness

NEAR the end of February, 1652, Milton became completely blind. On February 17, he still possessed sufficient vision to sign the Oldenburg safeguard; but on March 6 Mylius wrote in his diary that Milton had lost "all his sight." In a letter to Philaras, the Athenian physician, dated September 28, 1654, Milton wrote as follows: "It is ten years, I think, more or less, since I felt my sight getting weak and dull . . . if I began, as usual, to read anything, I felt my eyes at once thoroughly pained, and shrinking from the act of reading, but refreshed after moderate bodily exercise. If I looked at a lit candle, a kind of iris seemed to snatch it from me. Not very long after, a darkness coming over the left part of my left eye (for that eye became clouded some years before the other) removed from my vision all objects situated on that side . . . while yet a little sight remained, when first I lay down in bed, and turned myself to either side, there used to shine out a copious glittering light from my shut eyes; then . . . as my sight grew less from day to day, colours proportionately duller would burst from them, as with a kind of force and audible shot from within . . . the darkness which is perpetually before me, by night as well as by day, seems always nearer to a whitish than to a blackish, and such that, when the eye rolls itself, there is admitted, as through a small chink, a certain little trifle of light."

91

92

# Milton Under the Protectorate

## 93. Dissolution of the Rump

On April 20, 1653, hearing from General Thomas Harrison that the Rump Parliament was hurrying through a bill of election that would have continued the existing members in office, Cromwell summoned a guard of soldiers and caused them to be stationed at the doors of the House of Commons. Entering the House, Cromwell took his seat and waited: the bill was still under discussion. Fifty-three members were present, among them great personalities of the Commonwealth: Sir Henry Vane, Sir Peter Wentworth, Algernon Sidney, Bulstrode Whitelocke, Henry Marten, Colonel John Hutchinson. Finally Cromwell said to Harrison: "This is the time: I must do it." He rose as if to speak to the question. After some praise for the Rump's achievements, his tone changed: he attacked the members for their injustices, their self-interest, their desire to perpetuate themselves. He put on his hat, walked up and down, stamped

93A

93B

his feet. Looking fixedly at Marten and Wentworth, he cried out, "Some of you are whoremasters," and then, "You are no Parliament!" To Harrison he cried, "Call them in; Call them in!" When Vane protested, Cromwell cried, "Sir Henry Vane! Sir Henry Vane! The Lord deliver me from Sir Henry Vane!" After the members had filed out, Cromwell's last act was to snatch the offending bill from the clerk's hand and put it under his cloak.

Milton was too closely identified with the Rump Parliament as an official of the Council of State to have been wholly sympathetic with Cromwell's abrupt and contemptuous dismissal. Nevertheless, however ambivalent his sympathies when Cromwell was named Protector under the new *Instrument of Government* in December, 1653, Milton continued to serve the new regime as Secretary of Foreign Tongues. The two men Milton most admired, however, John Bradshaw and Sir Henry Vane, no longer graced the sessions of the Council of State.

93c

## Joannis Miltoni

# ANGLI
### PRO
## POPULO ANGLICANO
# DEFENSIO
## SECUNDA.

Contra infamem libellum anonymum
cui titulus,

*Regii sanguinis clamor ad
coelum adverfus parri-
cidas Anglicanos.*

---

## LONDINI,
### Typis Neucomianis, 1654.

## 94. Milton's *Second Defence*

ON May 30, 1654, Milton sent forth his *Second Defence of the English People*, in which he calls the roll of his heroes, conspicuously including John Bradshaw and Robert Overton, now out of favor. Though Milton does not name Sir Henry Vane, he walks between the lines as the blind poet's ideal statesman. Milton's high praise of Bradshaw he was evidently eager to place on record, as well as his panegyric of Sir Thomas Fairfax, now withdrawn from public life. Though Milton has high praise for Cromwell, he also ad-

monishes him: repeal old laws, now useless or pernicious; let not civil and ecclesiastical powers "make harlots of each other"; allow freedom of speech to your enemies. Then Milton adds a significant note: "Many men has war made great whom peace makes small." While defending the English people for establishing their new republic, he also defends himself against Alexander More, whom he wrongly named as the author of *The Cry of the Royal Blood*. Milton's defense of his own life he embodies in a succession of autobiographical passages, the richest and most comprehensive in his writings, beginning, "I shall now tell who and whence I am."

## 95. Milton on the Vaudois Massacres

ON April 24, 1655, in two Piedmontese valleys of the Alps west of Turin, where the Vaudois inhabitants had been dissenters since the thirteenth century, some 150 women and children were tortured and killed by soldiers under the command of the Marquis of Pianezza. The news of the persecution spread like wildfire throughout England, uniting for the moment all Protestant sects from Anglican to Baptist and Quaker. A day of fasting and prayer was appointed for May 30 in London and June 14 in the country at large. Unprecedented collections of £38,000 were made to relieve the suffering of the Vaudois, Cromwell himself contributing £2,000. A special commissioner, Samuel Morland, was sent to the scene of the massacres to gather evidence and make a full report. As Secretary for Foreign Tongues Mil-

ton drafted letters of protest to the crowned heads of Europe. Privately he wrote as follows:

Avenge, O Lord, thy slaughtered saints, whose
   bones
  Lie scattered on the Alpine mountains cold,
  Ev'n them who kept thy truth so pure of old
  When all our fathers worshiped stocks and
   stones,
Forget not; in thy book record their groans
  Who were thy sheep, and in their ancient fold
  Slain by the bloody Piemontese that rolled
  Mother with infant down the rocks. Their
   moans
The vales redoubled to the hills, and they
  To heav'n. Their martyred blood and ashes sow
  O'er all th' Italian fields, where still doth sway
The triple tyrant, that from these may grow
  A hundredfold, who, having learnt thy way,
  Early may fly the Babylonian woe.

96A

## 96. The Death of Cromwell

EARLY in August, 1658, Cromwell was confined to his bed at Hampton Court with an illness defined by the physicians as "a bastard tertian ague." On August 20 George Fox saw him in Hampton Court Park, riding at the head of his guards; to Fox he looked already like a dead man. The fever returned; Cromwell was removed from Hampton Court to Whitehall. In his restless sleep his speech was full of "holy expressions," such as, "Lord, though I am a miserable and wretched creature, I am in Covenant with Thee through grace." When drink was offered him, he would say, *"It is not my design to drink or to sleep, but my design is to make what haste I can to be gone."* On September 3, anniversary of Dunbar and Worcester, London was visited by one of the most tumultuous storms of English history. At three in the afternoon, Oliver Cromwell breathed his last.

Near to
this place was buried
on 25 March 1960 the head of
OLIVER CROMWELL
Lord Protector of the Commonwealth of England, Scotland &
Ireland, Fellow Commoner
of this College 1616-7

96B

RICHARD Lord Protector of England Scotland & Ireland, and the Dominions & Territoryes therevnto belonging:

97

## 97. Dilemma of Richard Cromwell

WITHIN three hours after Oliver's death, September 3, 1658, Richard Cromwell was named Protector. In the first months that followed, the country was calm. The Council of State met regularly under the new Parliament, which had convened January 27, 1659. Assisted since 1657 by Andrew Marvell, Milton continued in his post as Latin Secretary. Lucy Hutchinson wrote that Richard "was gentle and virtuous, but became not greatness." Richard indeed had assumed an impossible role; likeable and appealing as he was, he possessed little of his father's magic over the wills of men. "I do love the person of the Lord Protector," said Haselrig. "I never saw nor heard either fraud or guile in him." Scott said, "If you think of a single person, I would sooner have him

than any man alive." Another member said, "The sweetness of his voice and language has won my heart." For the moment the illustrious generals who had helped Oliver to power, among them Fleetwood, Desborough, and Monk, stood by Richard, as did his brother Henry. But Richard was not strong enough to choose among the contrary advices whirling around him. Monk had written from Scotland, urging him to secure the friendship of the leading Presbyterian divines and bring members of the wealthy landowning gentry into the House of Lords. As events unfolded, the Lord Protector was torn between the desires of the army and the predominant wishes of his Parliament. When the Commons voted that the army should not hold a general council without permission of the Protector and both Houses of Parliament, Richard, after long reluctance, cast his lot with the army. On April 21, 1659, he dissolved the Parliament. Meanwhile, when Colonel Charles Howard and Colonel Dick Ingoldsby had offered to arrest the chief army leaders, Richard had declined, saying, "I will not have a drop of blood spilt for the preservation of my greatness, which is a burden to me."

## 98. Bridget Cromwell

ELDEST daughter of the Protector, Bridget was baptized August 5, 1624, at St. John's Church in Huntingdon. Her early life was a relatively happy one, free from strain until the outbreak of the Civil War. At age twenty-two, about a year after the battle of Naseby, Bridget was married to Henry Ireton, one of the heroes of that action, and much admired by her father. Within six months after the tragic death of Ireton in Irish warfare, Bridget married Charles Fleetwood (June 8, 1652). In the chaotic shifts of power and loyalty that followed her father's death, Bridget stood loyally by her husband. In December, 1659, "she came into the room where we were," wrote Ludlow, "and with tears began to lament the present condition of her husband, who, she said, had been always unwilling to do any thing in opposition to the Parliament." At times both she and her husband were torn between the wishes of the leading officers and those of her brother, the Protector. In personal life Bridget was tenaciously loyal to her brother Henry, Lord Deputy of Ireland, as well as to Richard. In letters to Henry her woman's heart struggled to bridge the gap between them. "I am very unfit and unapt to write, and yet I would not altogether neglect to stir up that affection which ought to be betwixt so near relations, and is very apt to decay. I blame none but myself."

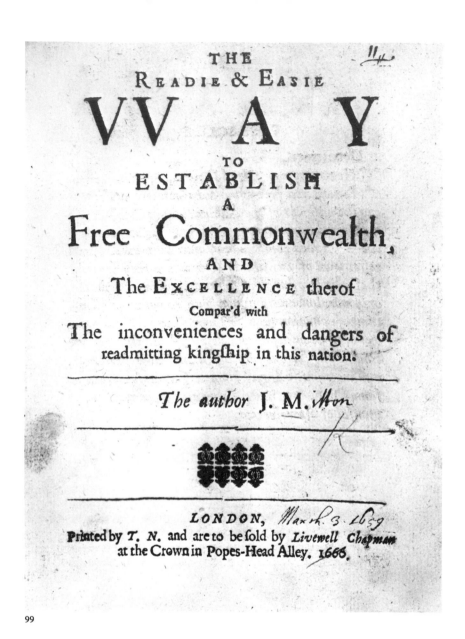

THE
READIE & EASIE
VVAY
TO
ESTABLISH
A
Free Commonwealth,
AND
The EXCELLENCE therof
Compar'd with
The inconveniences and dangers of
readmitting kingſhip in this nation.

The author J. M.*itton*

LONDON, *March. 3. 1659*
Printed by *T. N.* and are to be ſold by *Livewell Chapman*
at the Crown in Popes-Head Alley. 1666.

99

## 99. For the Good Old Cause: Milton's Last Stand

ON March 3, 1660, when the Commonwealth was toppling, many of its leaders already fleeing, and the restoration of monarchy less than two months away, Milton sent forth his *Readie & Easie Way to Establish a Free Commonwealth*. When attacked for his republican stand in Griffiths' *Fear of God and the King* (March 25), Harrington's *Censure of the Rota* (March 30), and L'Estrange's *No Blinde Guides* (April 20), Milton was probably already preparing a second edition of *The Readie & Easie Way*, which appeared, according to Masson's judgment, "some time in April." By this time the formal abolition of the Commonwealth was imminent (May 1) and many of its staunch defenders fleeing for their lives. Not so John Milton. "What I have spoken," he wrote, "is the language of that which is not call'd amiss *the good Old Cause*: if it seem strange to any, it will not seem more strange, I hope, then convincing to backsliders. Thus much I should perhaps have said though I were sure I should have spoken only to trees and stones; and had none to cry to, but with the Prophet, *O earth, earth, earth!* to tell the very soil it self, what her perverse inhabitants are deaf to." Thus Milton cried out from the depths of his spirit, his dreams for England in ruins, his great epic still a fragment, his greatest music unbreathed.

## By the King.

# A PROCLAMATION

For calling in, and suppreſſing of two Books written by *John Milton*; the one Intituled, *Johannis Miltoni Angli pro Populo Anglicano Defenſio, contra Claudii Anonymi aliàs Salmaſii, Defenſionem Regiam*; and the other in anſwer to a Book Intituled, *The Pourtraicture of his Sacred Majeſty in his Solitude and Sufferings.* And alſo a third Book Intituled, *The Obſtructors of Juſtice,* written by *John Goodwin.*

CHARLES R.

Hereas John Milton, late of Weſtminſter, in the County of Middleſex, hath Publiſhed in Print two ſeveral Books. The one Intituled, Johannis Miltoni Angli pro Populo Anglicano Defenſio, contra Claudii Anonymi, aliàs Salmaſii, Defenſionem Regiam. And the other in Anſwer to a Book Intituled, The Pourtraicture of his Sacred Majeſty in his Solitude and Sufferings. In both which are contained ſundry Treaſonable Paſſages againſt Us and Our Government, and moſt Impious endeavors to juſtifie the horrid and unmatchable Murther of Our late Dear Father, of Glorious Memory.

And whereas John Goodwin, late of Coleman-Street, London, Clerk, hath alſo publiſhed in Print, a Book Intituled, The Obſtructors of Juſtice, written in defence of his ſaid late Majeſty. And whereas the ſaid John Milton, and John Goodwin, are both fled, or ſo obſcure themſelves, that no endeavors uſed for their apprehenſion can take effect, whereby they might be brought to Legal Tryal, and deſervedly receive condigne puniſhment for their Treaſons and Offences.

Now to the end that Our good Subjects may not be corrupted in their Judgments, with ſuch wicked and Traitrous principles, as are diſperſed and ſcattered throughout the beforementioned Books, We, upon the motion of the Commons in Parliament now aſſembled, doe hereby ſtreightly charge and Command, all and every Perſon and Perſons whatſoever, who live in any City, Burrough, or Town Incorporate, within this our Kingdom of England, the Dominion of Wales, and Town of Berwick upon Tweed, in whoſe hands any of thoſe Books are, or hereafter ſhall be, That they, upon pain of Our high Diſpleaſure, and the conſequence thereof, do forthwith, upon publication of this Our Command, or within Ten days immediately following, deliver, or cauſe the ſame to be delivered to the Mayor, Baylifs, or other chief Officer or Magiſtrate, in any of the ſaid Cities, Burroughs, or Towns Incorporate, where ſuch perſon or perſons ſo live; or, if living out of any City, Burrough, or Town Incorporate, then to the next Juſtice of Peace adjoyning to his or their dwelling, or place of abode; or if living in either of Our Univerſities, then to the Vice-Chancellor of that Univerſity where he or they do reſide.

And in default of ſuch voluntary delivery, which we do expect in obſervance of Our ſaid Command, That then and after the time before limited, expired, the ſaid Chief Magiſtrate of all and every the ſaid Cities, Burroughs, or Towns Incorporate, the Juſtices of the Peace in their ſeveral Counties, and the Vice-Chancellors of Our ſaid Univerſities reſpectively, are hereby Commanded to Seize and Take, all and every the Books aforeſaid, in whoſe hands or poſſeſſion ſoever they ſhall be found, and certifie the names of the Offenders unto Our Privy Council.

And we do hereby alſo give ſpecial Charge and Command to the ſaid Chief Magiſtrates, Juſtices of the Peace, and Vice-Chancellors reſpectively, That they cauſe the ſaid Books which ſhall be ſo brought unto any of their hands, or ſeized or taken as aforeſaid, by vertue of this Our Proclamation, to be delivered to the reſpective Sheriffs of thoſe Counties where they reſpectively live, the firſt and next Aſſizes that ſhall after happen. And the ſaid Sheriffs are hereby alſo required, in time of holding ſuch Aſſizes, to cauſe the ſame to be publickly burnt by the hand of the Common Hangman.

And we do further ſtreightly Charge and Command, That no man hereafter preſume to Print, Vend, Sell, or Diſperſe any the aforeſaid Books, upon pain of Our heavy Diſpleaſure, and of ſuch further Puniſhment, as for their preſumption in that behalf, may any way be inflicted upon them by the Laws of this Realm.

Given at Our Court at *Whitehall* the 13th day of *Auguſt*, in the Twelfth year of Our Reign, 1660.

*LONDON,* Printed by *John Bill* and *Christopher Barker,* Printers to the Kings moſt Excellent Majeſty, 1660.

## 100. Milton Wanted by the King

WHEN Charles II entered London triumphantly on May 29, 1660, no opponent seemed more likely to lose his life as the king's enemy than John Milton. On May 1 the Commons had resolved unanimously that "the Government is, and ought to be, by King, Lords, and Commons." The cannons boomed, the bells rang, the bonfires flared. But some time in April, only days or weeks before the crucial resolution, Milton had issued the second edition of his *Readie & Easie Way*, with its brave and despairing cry, "*O earth, earth, earth!*" Since May 7 he had been in hiding in a friend's house in Bartholomew Close. Already, weeks before Charles' entrance into London, the House had been debating the names of persons to be excepted from the king's pardon; sixty-seven of the judges who had condemned Charles I were already among the names excepted. Milton seemed no more likely than they to be forgiven, certainly no more likely than Hugh Peters, who had already been arrested. Milton's old opponent William Prynne was in the House; for him the more exceptions to the king's pardon, the better. On June 16 the House moved that two books by Milton be called in and burned "by the hand of the common hangman," *A Defence of the English People* and *Eikonoklastes*, along with John Goodwin's book, *The Obstructors of Justice*. Both authors, asserted the king's proclamation (which did not appear in the printed broadside until August 13), had fled; they must be apprehended and brought to trial, whereby they may be punished for their "Treasons and Offences."

## 101. Milton Arrested and Jailed

ON June 16, 1660, the Commons resolved "That Mr. *Milton*, and Mr. *John Goodwin*, be forthwith sent for, in Custody, by the Serjeant-at-Arms attending this House." On August 13, the day of the king's *Proclamation* against Milton's books, he was still at large. On August 25 the Indemnity Bill was passed with good news for Milton and his friends; he was not one of those excepted from the king's forgiveness and hence not liable for execution. But meanwhile the House had not repealed its warrant for Milton's arrest, which apparently assumed his imprisonment as well, supervised by the Sergeant at Arms, Mr. James

Norfolke. Milton was apparently in prison during the first book burnings (his own books included on September 3-10), and during the executions of Harrison, Peters, Jones, and Axtell (October 13-19). The *Commons Journals* for December 17 record the following: "A Complaint being made that the Serjeant-at-Arms had demanded excessive Fees for the Imprisonment of Mr. *Milton*," it was ordered that "the Committee for Privileges . . . call Mr. *Milton* and the Serjeant before them; and to determine what is fit to be given the Serjeant for his Fees in this Case." The fees demanded were £150, a sum equivalent to £500 two centuries later. We learn that Andrew Marvell had come to Milton's rescue in the matter of Mr. Norfolke's exorbitant fees. Milton was even allowed to leave prison on Saturday, December 15, and spend Sunday with his family and friends, having been in confinement about three months.

## 102. How Did Milton Escape?

AMONG the men who helped save Milton from execution, Andrew Marvell in the House of Commons "acted vigorously in his behalf, and made

a considerable party for him." In the Commons also, according to Richardson, writing in 1734, General George Monk's brother-in-law, Sir Thomas Clarges, and his friend, Secretary Morrice, "manag'd Matters Artfully" for Milton. A still more important leader of the House (not mentioned by Richardson) was Arthur Annesley, who had indeed been the chief architect of the Restoration along with Monk. Annesley was a man of broad sympathies; like Monk he wanted as little bloodshed as possible. That Annesley's action was crucial is suggested by his intimate friendship for Milton after the Restoration; he cherished Milton's "society and converse" to the end of the blind poet's life. Diverse personalities in Commons and Lords cooperated to rescue Milton from the scaffold. Though unfriendly to Milton as a polemicist, Clarendon was a discerning admirer of literary genius. In 1650, when Sir William Davenant lay in a Commonwealth prison, Milton had obtained his release. According to Richardson's informant, Sir William now acted to save the blind poet. Milton owed his life, then, to a number of men working together skillfully in ways now impossible to measure in effect or unravel in sequence.

102B

102A

102C

103

# The Picture of the Good Old Cause drawn to the Life

In the *Effigies* of Master *PRAIS-GOD BAREBONE.*

WITH

Several Examples of Gods Judgements on some Eminent Engagers against Kingly Government.

1. Doriflaus, *one that had a great hand in the Kings murther, was ftab'd at the Hague in March* 1649. *when he was fent to treat with the Dutch in the name of the Free-State or Common-wealth of Eng-land.*

2. Anthony Afcham *ferved in the like manner at* Madrid *in* Spain, *near the fame time, being fent from the* Rump *on the like errand.*

3. Milton *that writ two Books againft the Kings, and* Salmafius *his Defence of Kings, ftruck total-ly blind, he being not much above* 40. *years old.*

4. Alderman Hoyle *of* York, *one of the Juncto, and high Court of Juftice, and (though he figned not the Kings Sentence) the fame day twelve moneth, the King was murthered, hanged himfelf in his Chamber at* Weftminfter.

5. Sir Gregory Norton *died raving mad, which by his Phyficians was not imputed to the diftem-per of his body, but a troubled, difquieted mind; He was one of the Kings Judges.*

*The Portraiture of M.*
*Praise God Barebone.*

6. Lockier, *once an Agitator in the Army, at his late Majefties pretended Triall, fpit Jew-like in the Kings Face, and likewife blew Tobacco-Afhes upon him ; Afterwards turned* Leveller, *and was fhot to death by his* Fellow-Rogues *in* Saint Pauls Church-yard.

7. Collonel Ven, *a Citizen of* London, *formerly a great Profeffour of Religion, but turned with the Times, was a Member of the* Rump, *a great En-gager againft Kingly Government, on* July *the* 7. 1650. *He going to bed as perfectly well and in health, as ever in his life, his Wife lying by him, he fell afleep by her immediately, and flept found-ly without complaint of the leaft diftemper,but the next morning about* 6 *a Clock, his Wife found him ftark dead by her, never having made the leaft groan,or fpoken one word to her fince the day be-fore ; and thus God banifhed him firft out of the Land of the Living.*

Many more inftances may be given, but I am loth to be too tedious.

104

## 103. The "Incomparable Lady Ranelagh"

ANOTHER friend who may have helped Milton escape was Lady Ranelagh, sister of the great Robert Boyle; her son, Richard Jones, had been one of Milton's students. For some years, from 1646 onward, Lady Ranelagh had been Milton's neighbor and frequent visitor to his house. In 1656 Milton wrote to Richard that Lady Ranelagh had stood for him "in the place of all kith and kin." In 1660 Lady Ranelagh, having long before separated from her husband, was keeping house for her renowned brother, entertaining many of the great royalist intellectuals of the time, herself a woman of remarkable gifts, admired by all who knew her. Men as different as Samuel Hartlib and Viscount Falkland had sought and cherished her friendship.

## 104. Abuse of Commonwealth Heroes

ON July 14, 1660, appeared a broadside called *Picture of the Good Old Cause*, castigating the enemies of royalty and dramatizing the punishments God was now inflicting upon them. Had not Alderman Hoyle hanged himself, and Gregory Norton, one of the king's judges, died "raving mad"? Then there was John Milton. Had he not been stricken blind (when little more than forty years old) for books against kingship and its great champion, Salmasius? The ridicule of Commonwealth heroes is ascribed ironically to Praisegod Barebones, preacher and prosperous leatherseller, who had served in Cromwell's Little Parliament. No lover of kingship, Barebones was vehemently opposed to the Restoration and suffered some months of imprisonment for his principles.

## 105. Hugh Peters on the Scaffold

ON October 16, 1660, Hugh Peters was executed as a regicide at Charing Cross. As with John Cook, whose execution he was forced to watch, Peters was first hanged, then cut down while still alive;

the executioner cut away his sex organs, burned his entrails before his eyes, then severed his head and hacked his body into quarters. According to the custom of the day, Peters' captors then set his head upon a pike at Westminster Hall and exposed his quarters on the city gates. The jeering crowd had watched eagerly, as they had watched Harrison on the 13th, for some sign of weakness or fear in Peters, chief chaplain of Cromwell's army. Peters indeed had feared his own fear; but he died with utter composure, the few words he tried to speak drowned by the hoots of the tumultuous crowd.

Lo heere ! the Dictates of a Dying : man !
Marke well his note! who like th'expiring Swan
Wisely præsaging hir approaching Doomb
Sings in soft charmes hir Epicædium .
Such Such are His ; who was a shining Lamp
Which though Extinguisht by a fatall Damp
Yet his Last = Breathings shall like Incense hurld
On sacred Altars, soe perfume the world,
That the Next, will admire, and out of doubt
Reuere that Torchlight, which this age, put out

## 106. The Execution of Sir Henry Vane

ON June 14, 1662, clad in black suit and cloak and a scarlet waistcoat, Sir Henry Vane was led forth to execution. Though reputed a timid man, Vane showed the audience such a serene and untroubled countenance that "he rather seemed a looker-on, than the person concerned in the Execution." To prevent his being heard by the multitude, his captors sounded trumpets and snatched his papers from his hands. Until the fatal blow Vane's face retained the utmost composure and serenity, and a royalist declared, "*He dyed like a Prince.*" As a knight Vane escaped the additional indignity of drawing and quartering. Thus died a Commonwealth hero dearest of all statesmen to Milton's heart, a man ripened, like Williams and Peters, in the bracing wilds of New England. Since Vane had not been a party to the trial of King Charles, he might indeed have escaped execution. To represent his own cause at his trial, however, he thrust aside all caution, all hope of reprieve, and spoke with the passion of a zealot. This action spelled his doom.

## 107. The Plague in London: 1665

IN April, 1665, as Milton was finishing *Paradise Lost*, the red spot plague broke out in London. By June the death rate per month had reached 590. In August some 20,046 succumbed to the dread pestilence; in September, 26,230. Plague pits were opened for mass burials, the death carts with their ghastly burdens and tolling bells moving through the streets day and night. The "great pit in Finsbury," mentioned by Defoe, was actually near Milton's house in Bunhill Fields. Knowing that death was near, many victims, wrote Defoe, crazed with pain and despair, "ran wrapped in blankets or rags and threw themselves in, and expired there before any earth could be thrown upon them." All families who could do so now fled from London, Milton and his daughters among them.

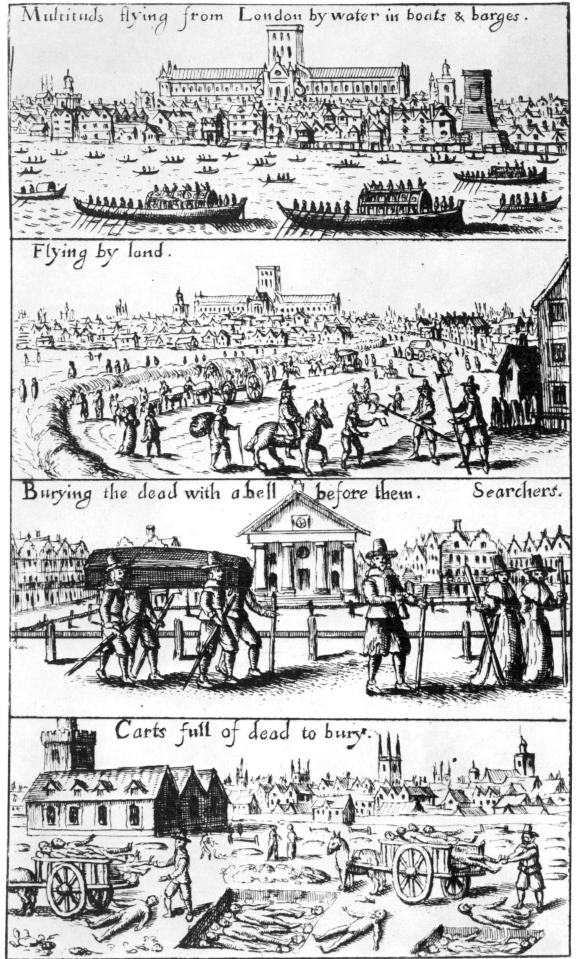

Multituds flying from London by water in boats & barges.

Flying by land.

Burying the dead with a bell before them.     Searchers.

Carts full of dead to bury.

108A

108B

## 108. Milton at Chalfont St. Giles

In July, 1665, Milton and his family moved to the village of Chalfont St. Giles, twenty-three miles from London, where his friend Thomas Ellwood had found him a pretty cottage with a lawn and a garden, only a mile from Ellwood's home. The cottage is the only dwelling still standing in which Milton lived, a house with leaded-pane windows, beamed ceilings, and two large fireplaces. When Milton and his family arrived at their new abode, Thomas Ellwood was not there to greet them. As a protesting Quaker, he had been imprisoned (along with Isaac Pennington the Younger) at Aylesbury jail. When released from prison, Ellwood came to the cottage to see his old teacher, who gave him a complete manuscript of his epic. After a time Ellwood returned the manuscript, saying, "Thou hast said much here of *Paradise lost*; but what hast thou to say on *Paradise found*?" According to Ellwood, Milton did not reply, but sat "some time in a Muse," then broke off the conversation and turned to another topic of discourse. Later, however, when Milton had returned to London (probably in February, 1666) he showed Ellwood the manuscript of *Paradise Regained*, and said to him, "*This is owing to you: for you put it into my Head, by the Question you put to me at Chalfont; which before I had not thought of.*" Whether or not *Paradise Regained* had its origin in Ellwood's suggestion remains a moot question to this day.

## 109. Friends in the Jordans Churchyard

Only a few miles from Chalfont St. Giles, on a winding rural road, stands the historic Jordans meeting house, of which Thomas Ellwood was a member. On the sloping lawn in front of the house one finds a number of simple gravestones, under which lie buried two men Milton knew: Thomas Ellwood himself, and Isaac Pennington the Younger, imprisoned in 1665 in Aylesbury jail. From the same Quaker community of Jordans, William Penn had migrated to America; he also lies buried in the churchyard, with Friends of an earlier generation.

## 110. Milton Completes *Paradise Lost*

By autumn, 1665, Milton had brought his great epic to a triumphant end, however tragic its theme. Three years before, by the last months of 1662, he had pushed his masterpiece as far forward as Book VII, dictating the lines day by day. "Half yet," he wrote, "remaines unsung." At this point Milton turned aside to comment on his own indomitable energy and mood:

> More safe I Sing with mortal voice, unchang'd
> To hoarce or mute, though fall'n on evil dayes,
> On evil dayes though fall'n, and evil tongues;
> In darkness, and with dangers compast round,
> And solitude; yet not alone, while thou
> Visit'st my slumbers Nightly, or when Morn
> Purples the East: still govern thou my Song,
> *Urania*, and fit audience find, though few.

The story of the creation that follows, though rich in detail, possesses that remarkable structural precision and classical restraint that only Milton's still flowering genius could call forth. Adam speaks to Raphael, asking him in effect, "How was this world created?" Then, step by step, the angel unfolds the creation of the universe out of "the vast immeasurable Abyss" of Chaos, which obeyed the command of the Son ("*Chaos* heard his voice"), the effective might of Jehovah himself:

> In his hand
> He took the golden Compasses, prepar'd
> In Gods Eternal store, to circumscribe
> This Universe, and all created things:
> One foot he center'd, and the other turn'd
> Round through the vast profunditie obscure,
> And said, thus farr extend, thus farr thy bounds,
> This be thy just Circumference, O World.

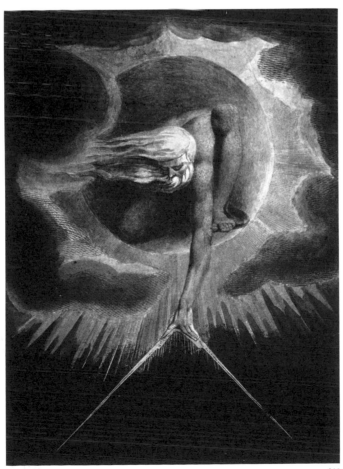

## 111. Milton and Raphael's *Adam and Eve*

Of the great paintings depicting the story of Adam and Eve, none is so dramatic as that of Raphael, which Milton probably saw during one of his two visits to Rome in the Vatican *Stanza Della Segnatura*. No scene in *Paradise Lost* portrays Adam and Eve with the serpent between them, looking down, as in Raphael's masterpiece. Moreover, though the face of the serpent might be either masculine or feminine, Raphael undoubtedly represents Satan here as feminine, in keeping with the tradition the artist inherited from his predecessors, few of whom represent Satan as masculine. For purposes of his great epic Milton needed a Satan surpassingly heroic, a figure of such epic strength as to challenge the might of God's own assembled angels. In so representing Satan, Milton unhesitatingly rejected the tradition of his predecessors in the field of both poetry and painting.

111

112

## 112. Milton and the Tawny Lion

"In no part of his writings," writes Coleridge in *Table Talk*, "does Milton take any notice of the great painters of Italy, nor, indeed, of painting as an art; while every other page breathes his love and taste for music." Yet in one passage, asserts Coleridge, in the story of the creation in Book VII, "Milton has certainly copied the fresco of the Creation in the Sistine Chapel." [Coleridge made an error here: Raphael's painting appears in the Loggia.] Coleridge then quotes these lines:

> Now half appeer'd
> The Tawnie Lion, pawing to get free
> His hinder parts, then springs as broke from
>     Bonds,
> And Rampant shakes his Brinded main.

When we look today at Raphael's painting, we see indeed the brinded mane of the lion as he emerges from the earth beneath the right hand of the Creator; but we do not see his paws working to free his body. A small pup of a lion, to the right of the Creator, with his right paw raised, better fits Milton's image of this bit of action in the painting, which he may have called up from his memories of twenty-five years before.

## 113. The Creation of Eve

In his dialogue with God in Book VIII of *Paradise Lost*, Adam bemoans his lonely state, reminding his Maker that each animal has his mate: but not man. After a brief resistance to Adam's sugges-tion, in which God reminds Adam that he, the Lord, is himself happy without a mate, the Almighty says, "I, ere thou spak'st, knew it not good for man to be alone." When Adam, "dazzled and spent," lies down, he sees as in a trance, the creation of Eve. The Lord

> Stooping opened my left side, and took
> From thence a rib, with cordial spirits warm,
> And life-blood streaming fresh; wide was the
>     wound,
> But suddenly with flesh filled up and healed.
> The rib he formed and fashiond with his hands;
> Under his forming hands a creature grew,
> Man-like, but different sex, so lovely fair
> That what seemed fair in all the world seemed
>     now
> Mean, or in her summed up, in her contained
> And in her looks, which from that time infused
> Sweetness into my heart, unfelt before,
> And into all things from her air inspired
> The spirit of love and amorous delight.

## 114. Adam and Eve Expelled from Paradise

NEAR the end of *Paradise Lost*, after the angel has unfolded to him the prophetic panorama of mankind's sufferings to come, Adam sees in the distance a flaming sword held aloft by one of the angelic guards. The sword "waves fiercely round": a signal the angels must depart. The archangel Michael says to Adam:

> We may no longer stay: go, waken *Eve*;
> Her also I with gentle Dreams have calm'd
> Portending good, and all her spirits compos'd
> To meek submission.

Descending the hill of Paradise, Adam and the archangel walk toward the bower where Eve has been sleeping. There they find her already awake and ready, cheerful in mien and composed in spirit. The angelic guard begins its march:

> High in Front advanc't,
> The brandisht Sword of God before them blaz'd
> Fierce as a Comet.

The archangel takes Adam and Eve each by the hand and leads them to the Eastern Gate, down the cliff and to the plain; then he disappears. Adam and Eve "with wandring steps and slow, through *Eden* took thir solitarie way."

## 115. The Great Fire of London: 1666

ON September 2, 1666, the Great Fire of London began its ravages, and continued for three days, reducing two-thirds of the city to ruins and ashes. The fire toppled the vast bulk of St. Paul's and brought down a hundred other towers and steeples. All told, the fire laid desolate 436 square acres "from the Tower to Temple Bar, and from the river to Aldersgate, Cripplegate, and Moorgate." Within the walls all that remained of London was a sliver of the east side. By Masson's analysis the fire came within a quarter mile of Milton's house on Artillery Walk. Cheapside and Bread Street lay in ruins, including his own house of the Spread Eagle, the only real estate he had until now possessed.

Paradise lost.
A
POEM
Written in
TEN BOOKS
By *JOHN MILTON.*

Licensed and Entred according
to Order.

LONDON
Printed, and are to be sold by *Peter Parker*
under *Creed* Church neer *Aldgate* ; And by
*Robert Boulter* at the *Turks Head* in *Bishopsgate-street* ;
And *Matthias Walker*, under St. *Dunstons* Church
in *Fleet-street*, 1667.

116A

## 116. The Publication of *Paradise Lost*

IN EARLY 1667 the manuscript of *Paradise Lost* was approved for publication by Reverend Thomas Tomkyns, one of the official licensers of the press. On April 27 Milton made an agreement with Samuel Simmons, a printer (possibly a relative of Matthew Simmons), by which for a payment to Milton of five pounds Simmons agreed to publish thirteen hundred copies of *Paradise Lost*, which would henceforth become his property. The book was entered in the *Stationers' Registers* on August 20, when presumably it was almost ready for distribution to the various bookstalls throughout the city.

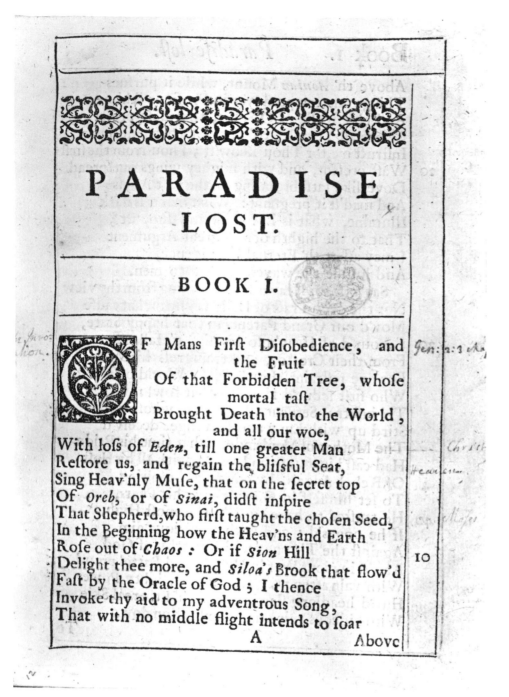

## 117. The Reception of *Paradise Lost*

MILTON'S great epic won almost immediate renown among discriminating readers. Between 1300 and 1500 copies were printed in the first edition; but not all copies were bound. As the demand for the poem increased among the booksellers, the printer (Samuel Simmons) bound up new batches of the book. According to Masson, there were at least nine such bindings of the first edition of *Paradise Lost*: two appeared in 1667, four in 1668, and three in 1669. Milton cooperated with the printer to make his epic more appealing to the learned public. In the fourth issue he inserted the "Arguments" in succession for the vari-

W. Dolle. sculpsit.

Ioannis Miltoni Effigies
Ætat. 63. 1671.

117A

ous ten books. This innovation was followed by "The Verse," explaining to the curious reader (as the printer wrote) "why the Poem Rimes not." In the second edition of 1674, the epic appeared for the first time in twelve books instead of ten; also for the first time an "Argument" preceded each book. Laudatory verses by Andrew Marvell and Samuel Barrow, with an engraved portrait of Milton, were inserted in the second edition. Milton's name was becoming a

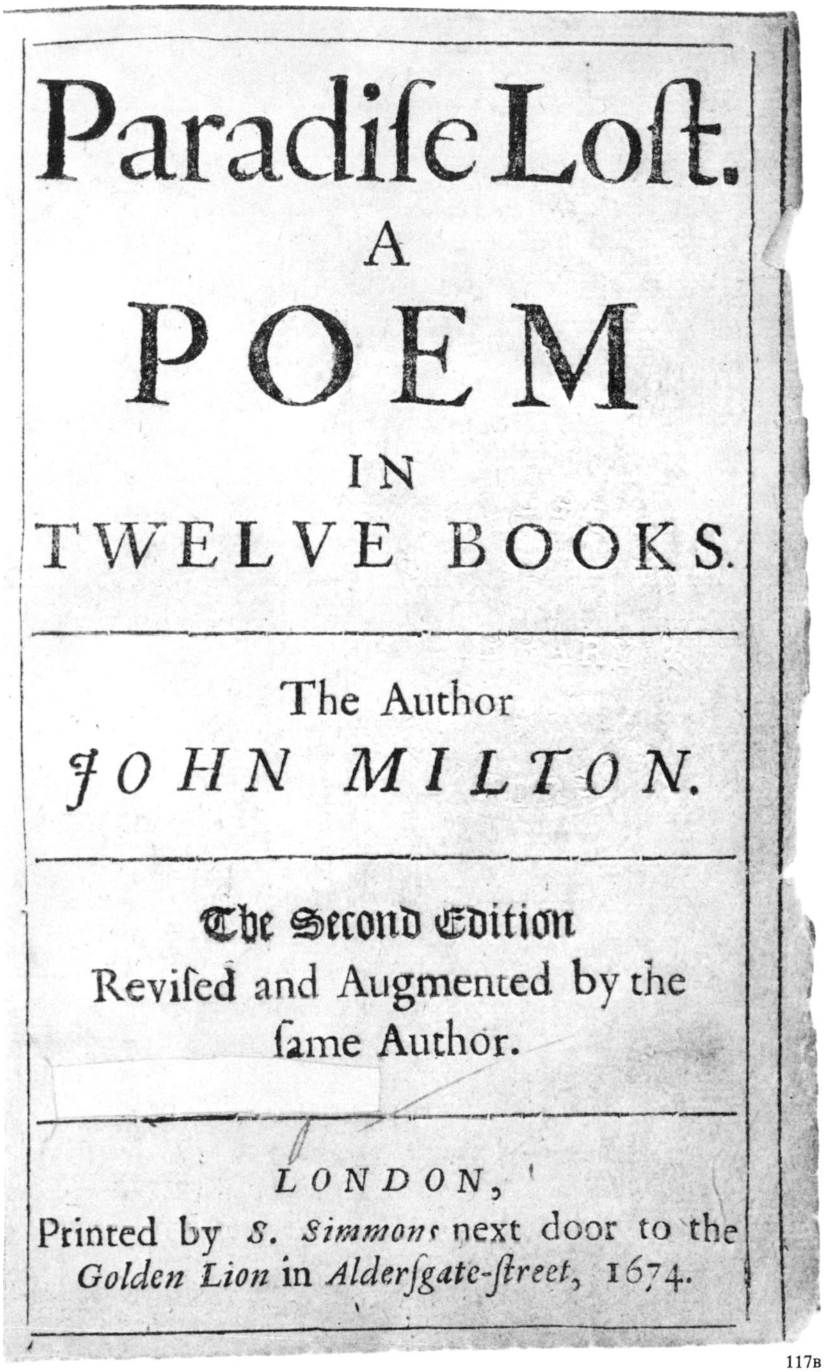

## Paradife Loft.

## A
## POEM
### IN
### TWELVE BOOKS.

The Author
*JOHN MILTON.*

𝔗𝔥𝔢 𝔖𝔢𝔠𝔬𝔫𝔡 𝔈𝔡𝔦𝔱𝔦𝔬𝔫
Revifed and Augmented by the
fame Author.

LONDON,
Printed by *S. Simmons* next door to the
*Golden Lion* in *Alderfgate-ftreet*, 1674.

117B

legend. For his poetic genius many royalists forgave his hatred of kings. Richardson tells the story of George Hungerford (an elderly member of Parliament) about Sir John Denham: "*Denham* came into the House one Morning with a Sheet, Wet from the Press, in his Hand. What have you there, Sir *John*? Part of the Noblest Poem that ever was Wrote in Any Language, or in Any Age. This was *Paradise Lost*." And Dryden said, "*This Man Cuts us All Out, and the Ancients too.*"

118A

## 118. The Publication of *Paradise Regained* and *Samson*

ON September 20, 1670, a little over two months before Milton's sixty-second birthday, *Paradise Regained* and *Samson* were entered in the *Stationers' Registers*. Milton intended *Regained* to be a philosophical dialogue, like the book of Job. As Job was tempted, so Christ is tempted, in nine separate scenes, by the wily Satan. But *Regained* lacks the fire of Job's language. It is bare, simple, unadorned, deficient in vivid imagery, figures of speech, magnificent flights of poetic music. A main element of Milton's genius, the mingling of Greek and Hebraic art and thought is only weakly represented in the narrative. The very portrayal of Jesus as the embodiment of Hebraic religious genius excluded in the main Milton's resources in Greek literature. Moreover, *Paradise Regained* deals with victory, not defeat, a theme that could not stir his deepest poetic energies. Nor did the imaginative compassion of the character of Jesus find a deep response in Milton's

# PARADISE REGAIN'D.

## A POEM.

### In IV BOOKS.

To which is added

AMSON AGONISTES.

The Author

*JOHN MILTON.*

LONDON,

inted by *J. M.* for *John Starkey* at the
*Mitre* in *Fleetſtreet,* near *Temple-Bar.*
MDCLXXI.

# SAMSON AGONISTES,

## A DRAMATIC POEM.

The Author

*JOHN MILTON.*

*Ariſtot. Poet. Cap. 6.*

Τραγῳδία μίμησις πράξεως σπεδαίας, &c.

*Tragædia eſt imitatio actionis ſeriæ,* &c. *Per miſericordiam &*
*metum perficiens talium affectuum luſtrationem.*

LONDON,

Printed by *J. M.* for *John Starkey* at the
*Mitre* in *Fleetſtreet,* near *Temple-Bar.*
MDCLXXI.

118B     118C

spirit. As in Job, the main theme of *Regained* is resistance to temptations Satan presents to Jesus. But temptation in itself does not possess the stature of tragic dilemma.

In *Samson Agonistes* Milton made choice of a theme ideally suited to his miraculous resources. For almost twenty years he had lived in total darkness, a small part of that time in prison or under house arrest, listening for the knock on the door, hearing the derisive shouts of the Cavalier bullies, enduring the deaths of friends who had stood staunchly for the Good Old Cause. None but a blind man could have written:

> Why was the sight
> To such a tender ball as th' eye confin'd?
> So obvious and so easie to be quench't,
> And not as feeling through all parts diffus'd,
> That she might look at will through every pore?

It was easy for Milton to imagine Samson's plight, to give him intellectual qualities not present in the Biblical hero, easy too for Milton to picture Samson betrayed by a woman. Further, Milton's long love of and familiarity with Greek literature, especially tragedy, now bore fruit. The two sides of his deep learning, the Hebraic and the Greek, were joined in unique achievement, as in *Paradise Lost.*

## 119. The Last Months of Milton's Life

IN WARM weather, wrote Richardson, Milton "used to sit in a grey coarse cloth coat at the door of his house, near Bunhill Fields, without Moorgate . . . to enjoy the fresh air, and so, as well as in his room, received the visits of people of distinguished parts." His voice was still musical, his bearing resolute, his manner stately and affable. Hearing a lady sing well, he said, "Now will I swear, this lady is handsome." In his last years his hands and fingers increasingly were "gouty and with chalk-stones." If only he could be free from gouty pain, he said, "his blindness would be tolerable." At the end of July, 1674, when Christopher Milton went to Bunhill for a visit with his brother, Milton spoke of his death as a possibility before Christopher's return to London. Though the poet referred to his "unkind children," he reminded Christopher that they would receive that portion due him from his first wife's father, a sum, we later find, of a thousand pounds. At the end of July Milton was still up and about, but by November he was stricken again with "severe gout fever." On Sunday, November 8, late at night, Milton's end came with "so little pain that the time of his expiring was not perceived by those in the room." On Thursday, November 12, the poet was buried beside his father at the church of St. Giles, Cripplegate, with a funeral service carried out according to the ritual of the Church of England.

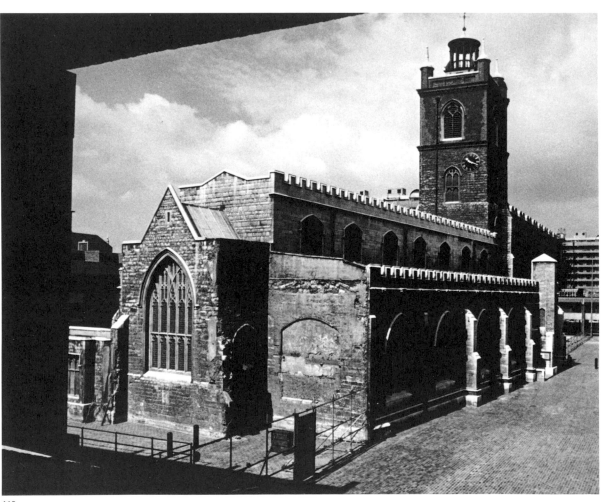

119A

# Chronology of Main Events

1608. Milton born December 9.

1620? Became a student in St. Paul's School; graduated in 1624 or 1625.

1625. Enrolled as lesser pensioner at Christ's College, February 12. Probably took up residence on April 9.

1625. Ascension of Charles I, March 27; Charles then twenty-four years old.

1628. The Petition of Right, March 26.

1629. Degree of B.A., March 26. *The Nativity Ode*, December 25.

1632. Degree of M.A., July 3. Settled at Hammersmith in July. First published poem, "On Shakespear. 1630." *Arcades*.

1633. Laud made Archbishop of Canterbury.

1634. *Comus* performed at Ludlow, September 29.

1635. Settled at Horton with his family.

1637. *Lycidas*, November.

1638. May (?). Left England for tour of the Continent. Paris, Florence, Siena, Rome, Naples, Lucca, Venice, Geneva.

1639. July (?). Milton returned to England.

1640. Began teaching his two nephews, John and Edward Phillips. Long Parliament summoned. Impeachment of Laud and Strafford.

1641- *Of Reformation*, May, 1641; *Of Prelatical*
42. *Episcopacy*, July; *Animadversions*, July; *Reason of Church-Government*, January or February, 1642; *Apology against a Pamphlet*, April, 1642.

1641. Execution of Strafford. Irish Rebellion. *Grand Remonstrance*.

1642. Married Mary Powell, who left him within a few months, returned to her parents. Added more pupils to his household.

1643. *Doctrine and Discipline*, August 1.

1644. *Doctrine and Discipline*, 2nd. edition, February 2. *Of Education*, June 5. *Martin Bucer*, July 15. *Areopagitica*, November 24.
Battles of Marston Moor and Newbury.

1645. *Tetrachordon* and *Colasterion*, March 4. Reconciliation with Mary Powell, July or August.

Battle of Naseby. Success of New Model Army.

1645- First volume of poems published: *Poems*
46. *of Mr. John Milton.*

1646. Birth of Anne, first child, July 29. Surrender of Oxford. Powell family with the Milton family for a brief time.

1647. Death of Milton's father, March 15. Milton gave up teaching. Moved to a smaller house in High Holborn.
King Charles's flight to Carisbrook, November. London occupied by Cromwell's army.

1648. Second child, Mary, born October 25.

1649. Execution of Charles I, January 30. Abolition of monarchy, January 30. The Commonwealth proclaimed, January 30.
*Tenure of Kings and Magistrates*, February. Appointed Secretary of Foreign Tongues to Council of State, February. Assigned chambers in Whitehall, March. *Eikonoklastes*, October.

1651. Birth of third child, John, March 16. Death of infant shortly after. *Defence of the English People*, February. Moved from Whitehall lodgings to Petty France, Westminster.

1652. Total blindness, February. Daughter Deborah born, May 2. Death of Mary Powell, May 5.

1653. Dissolution of the Rump Parliament, April 20. Cromwell named Protector.

1654. *Second Defence* published, May 30.

1655. *Defence of Himself* published, August 8.

1656. Marriage to Katherine Woodcock, November 12.

1657. Daughter born, October 19.

1658. Deaths of Katherine Woodcock and infant daughter, February and March. Began *Paradise Lost*, May (?).
Death of Cromwell, September 3.

1658? Began *Christian Doctrine*.

1659. *Treatise of Civil Power*, February 16. *Considerations Touching the Likeliest Means*, August. *Proposalls of Certain Expedients* (?) *Letter to a Friend*, October 20.

1660. *Readie & Easie Way*, March 3. *The Present Means* (letter to Monk) March (?). *Brief Notes on a Late Sermon*, April. Second edition, *Readie & Easie Way*, April (?).

Restoration of the monarchy, May. Milton in hiding in Bartholomew Close. Proclamation by the King against Milton. Arrest of Milton.

1663. Marriage to Elizabeth Minshull, February 24.

1665. The plague in London. Milton moved to house in Chalfont St. Giles, July. Completed *Paradise Lost*.

1666. Great Fire of London.

1667. Publication of *Paradise Lost*, August (?).

1669. *Accidenc't Commenc'd Grammar*.

1670. *History of Britain* published.

1671. *Paradise Regained* and *Samson Agonistes* published.

1672. *Art of Logic* published.

1673. Enlarged edition of *Poems* published.

1674. *Paradise Lost* published, second edition. *Familiar Letters* published.

Death of Milton of the gout, November 8; buried in St. Giles, Cripplegate.

# Index

*Agreement of the People*: 74, 75
Annesley, Arthur: 102
Arnold, Christopher: 91
Ashburnham, John: 54
Aubrey, John: 1, 14, 41

Bacon, Francis: 5, 61
Barberini, Cardinal Francesco: 32, 33
Baroni, Leonora: 33
Bastwick, John: 44
Battle of Naseby: 66, 69
Baxter, Richard: 67
Bell, Robert: 10
Blackfriars Theatre: 5, 21
Bonmatthei, Benedetto: 29
Bradshaw, John: 83
Bread Street: 5, 14, 21
Brennecke, Ernest: 6
Bridgewater, Earl of: 23
Buckingham, Duke of: 9
Burton, Henry: 44
Butts, Dr. Henry: 19

Cambridge University: 7
Carey, Lucius, Viscount Falkland: 56
Chappell, William: 14
Charles I: 10, 51, 53, 54, 66, 69, 70, 71, 76, 78, 79, 83, 84
Christ's College: 2, 10, 11, 12, 15, 26
Churches: Christ's Church, Oxford: 6; St. Giles Cripplegate: 5; St. Mary Le Bow: 5; St. Paul's: 5, 7
Clarges, Sir Thomas: 102
Clarke, Deborah (*see* family)
*Clarke Papers*: 74
Clarke, Sir Simon: 20
Coles, John: 7
Coltellini, Agostino: 29
Comenius, John Amos: 61
Cook, John: 105
Cromwell, Bridget: 98
Cromwell, Henry: 98
Cromwell, Oliver: 5, 45, 49, 55, 63, 66, 67, 69, 77, 78, 80, 83, 88, 89, 96
Cromwell Richard: 97

Dante, Aligheri: 30
Dati, Carlo: 29, 30
Davenant, Sir William: 102
Digges, Leonard: 21
Diodati, Charles: 10, 14, 21
*Dolefull Lamentation of Cheapside Cross*: 52
Donne, John: 5

Fairfax, Sir Thomas: 66
Faithorne, William: 3
Felton, John: 9

Gaddi, Jacopo: 29
Galileo: 31
Gardiner, Sir Thomas: 41
Gill, Alexander, the elder: 7, 8
Gill, Alexander, the younger: 8, 9
Goodwin, John: 100
Great Seal, flight of: 53
Griffith, Dr. Matthew: 99
Grotius, Hugo: 27

Hall, Joseph, Bishop: 42
Hampden, John: 45, 47, 51
Hanford, James Holly, "Chronology of Milton's Private Studies": 22
Harefield: 23
Harrington, James: 99
Harrison, Colonel Thomas: 75
Hartlib, Samuel, friend of Milton: 61, 103
Harvey, William: 5
Haselrig, Sir Arthur: 97
Henrietta Maria, Queen of England: 51
High Court of Justice: 82
Hobson the Carrier: 20
Holland, Hugh: 21
Holsten, Lucas: 32
Hopton, Sir Ralph: 54
Huchinson, Lucy: 97
Hyde, Edward, Earl of Clarendon: 56

Ireton, General Henry: 66, 83

James I: 10

Janssen, Cornelius: 1
Jones, Richard: 103
Jonson, Ben: 5, 21
Joyce, George: 73

King, Edward: 26
King's College, Cambridge University: 10

Laud, Archbishop William: 9, 47, 65
Lawes, Henry: 5, 23, 24
Lenthall, William: 69
Lilburne, John: 46
Lilburne, Robert: 75
Littleton, Edward, Lord Keeper of the Great Seal: 53
Loggan, David: 11
Ludlow Castle: 24
Lyttleton, Edward, Lord Keeper: 53

Masson, David: 3, 12, 31, 37, 38, 40, 54
Milton, John (biographical): as in four portraits: 1,2,3,4; Bread Street neighborhood: 5; a dutiful son: 6; a student at St. Paul's: 7; and Alexander Gill, the Younger: 9; at Christ's College: 10; and Diodati: 14; at eighteen: 14; at twenty: 16; at twenty-four, on Shakespeare: 21
    family: John (father of the poet): 6, 25; Sarah (mother): 25; Christopher (brother of the poet): 25, 119; Anne (sister): 25, 41; Mary Powell (first wife): 59; children: Anne (oldest daughter), Mary (second daughter); Deborah (third daughter): 59; John (only son, who died in infancy): 59; Katherine Woodcock (second wife of the poet), who died at the birth of her infant daughter, also named Katherine: 59; Elizabeth Minshull (third wife of the poet), who survived him many years: 59

friendships: Annesley, Arthur: 102; Arnold, Christopher: 91; Bonmatthei, Benedetto: 29; Bradshaw, John: 83; Dati, Carlo: 29, 30; Diodati, Charles: 10, 14, 21; Diodati, John: 40; Ellwood, Thomas: 109; Fleetwood, Charles: 97; Gaddi, Jacopo: 29 Galileo: 31; Grotius, Hugo: 27; Hartlib, Samuel: 61, 103; Holsten, Lucas: 32; Jones, Richard: 103; Mansus, Joannes Baptista: 34; Marvell, Andrew: 97, 101, 102; Mylius, Hermann: 92; Overton, Robert: 94; Phillips, Edward: 39; Ranelagh, Lady: 41, 103; Vane, Sir Henry: 93, 94; Wotton, Sir Henry: 27; Young, Thomas: 1

Hammersmith and Horton, 1632-1638: entries in the *Commonplace Book*: 22; *Arcades* at Harefield: 23; growth of creative confidence in *Comus*: 24; death of Milton's mother, 25; "Lycidas": 26

Milton's European Tour, 1639-1640: In Paris: meeting with Grotius and Lord Scudamore: 27; in Florence: Dati, Gaddi, Bonmatthei: 29; meeting with Galileo: 31; Lucas Holsten in Rome: 32; Leonora Baroni in Rome; 33; Manso in Naples: 34; visit to Vallombrosa: 37; from Venice to Geneva: 39-40

Milton and the Civil War: Bishops under fire: 42, 48; Milton's anti-prelatical tracts: 42; marriage: 58; and the divorce heresy: 60; Milton on educational reform: 62; Puritan victories: Marston Moor: 63; Naseby: 66; *Poems of Mr. John Milton*: 72; Preston: 80; *The Tenure*: Milton against kingship: 85; execution of Charles I: 84; Milton as Latin Secretary: 86

Milton under the Protectorate, 1653-1658: *Second Defence*: 94;

sonnet on the Vaudois massacres: 95; death of Cromwell: 96; Richard Cromwell as Protector: 97; Bridget Cromwell: 98

Milton in the Restoration: wanted by the king: 100; under arrest: 101; escapes execution: 102; and Lady Ranelagh: 103; Hugh Peters and Henry Vane on scaffold, 105, 106; the London Plague, 1665: 107; at Chalfont St. Giles: 108; completes *Paradise Lost*: 110; Great Fire of London, 1666: 115; *Paradise Lost* published: 116; reception of great epic: 117; appearance of *Paradise Regained* and *Samson*: 118; last months of Milton's life: 119

Milton, John (writings): *Ad Patrem*: 6; *Animadversions*: 42; *Apology against a Pamphlet*: 42; *Arcades*: 23; *Areopagitica*: 31, 64, 67; *Christian Doctrine*: 59; *Commonplace Book*: 22; *Comus*: 24; *Defence of the English People*: 87, 100; *Doctrine and Discipline of Divorce*: 58, 60, 62, 64; *Of Education*: 62; *Eikonoklastes*: 50; *Elegy I*: 14; *Elegy VII*: 16; *History of Britain*: 4; "Hobson the Carrier": 20; Italian sonnets: 38; *Judgment of Martin Bucer*: 60; "Lycidas": 26; *Mansus*: 35; *Obsequies to the memorie of Mr Edward King*: 26; "On the Morning of Christ's Nativity": 2, 18. "On Shakespear. 1630": 5, 21; *Paradise Lost*: 3, 7, 18, 32, 36, 37, 113; *Paradise Regained*: 18; *Poems* (1645): 2, 30, 43, 72; *Of Prelatical Episcopacy*: 42; *Prolusions*: "An attack on the Scholastic Philosophy": 13; "On the Harmony of the Spheres": 13; "Whether Day or Night is More Excellent": 13; *Readie & Easie Way*: 57; *Reason of Church-Government*: 42; *Of Reformation*: 42; *Samson Agonistes*: 118; *Second Defence of the English People*: 5, 25, 27, 28, 29, 32, 37, 38, 40, 42, 57; *Tenure of Kings and Magistrates*: 85

Oxford (Christ Church): 6, 7

Peterhouse, Cambridge University: 10
Peters, Hugh: 100
Phillips, Edward: 41
plague at Cambridge, 19
Plato (on habits of dress), 29
Port, Robert: 10
Preston, battle of: 80
Pride, Colonel Thomas: 81
Prynne, William: 44
Pym, John: 47, 49, 51

Ranelagh, Lady: 41
Ravenscroft, Thomas: 6
Richardson, Jonathan: 4
Rous, John: 43

St. Paul's School: 1, 5, 7, 9
Shakespeare, William: 1, 5, 21
Smythe, Oliver: 8
Sound, William, 8
Spenser, Edmund: 8, 18
Stanton, St. John: 6
Strafford, Thomas: 49, 50, 51
street cries of London: 17
Sturbridge Fair: 12
Svoliati Academy: 29, 37

Tabor, Mr., Registrar at Christ's College: 10
Tasso: 33, 34; and Leonora: 33
Trinity College, Cambridge: 10
Trinity College, Oxford: 9
Trumpington Street, Cambridge: 20

Vertue, George: 4

Warwick, Sir Philip: 45, 54
Wood, Anthony à: 9
Wotton, Sir Henry: 27

Young, Thomas: 1